SCM PAPERBACKS

now published

MEN OF UNITY *by Stephen Neill*
THE MIND OF JESUS *by William Barclay*
CRUCIFIED AND CROWNED *by William Barclay*
ST PAUL AND THE GOSPEL OF JESUS *by Charles E. Raven*
THE BIBLE IN THE AGE OF SCIENCE *by Alan Richardson*
INTRODUCING THE CHRISTIAN FAITH *by A. M. Ramsey,*
Archbishop of Canterbury
THE BRITISH CHURCHES TODAY *by Kenneth Slack*

future titles will include

CHRISTIAN DEVIATIONS: THE CHALLENGE OF THE SECTS
by Horton Davies
WE THE PEOPLE *by Kathleen Bliss*
WHY READ THE OLD TESTAMENT? *by Erik Routley*
JESUS AS THEY SAW HIM *by William Barclay*
DESPATCH FROM NEW DELHI *by Kenneth Slack*

books which everyone can learn from and keep

KENNETH SLACK

The British Churches
Today

SCM PRESS LTD
BLOOMSBURY STREET LONDON

FIRST PUBLISHED 1961
© KENNETH SLACK 1961
PRINTED IN HOLLAND BY
DRUKKERIJ HOLLAND N.V. AMSTERDAM

CONTENTS

To
Nicholas, Rosalind
and Timothy

INTRODUCTION

'There are in England sixty different religious sects, but only one sauce.' *Francesco Caraccioli* (1752-1799).

THE United States of America has the greatest popular reputation for a fantastic variety of Christian denominations and sects. The diversity of its immigrants, bringing with them the churchmanship of their nations, and the hospitality of its shores in earlier days to those who had rejected that churchmanship to follow other leadings of the Spirit, have both contributed to this variety. Nevertheless in proportion to their land area the British Isles show a hardly less luxuriant growth of varied denominational allegiance.

In one respect at least the British scene outrivals the American. The latter has but one Church-State relationship. There is as complete a division between the two as is compatible with the Church being a body subject to the normal law of the land. Thus, for example, religion is not taught in any of the schools provided by the State. In the British Isles there are at least three different Church-State relationships. In England the Church of England is by law established and indeed is, in the last resort, subject to Parliament. It is a State Church in that sense, and is, of course, episcopal in government. In Scotland, as we shall see in a later chapter, as a result of a long struggle the national recognition of Christianity has been established on a far more defensible basis. There the Church of Scotland, which is Presbyterian, is free from state control but regarded as the national Church. In the Republic of Ireland the Church of Rome is specially recognised. It may further be added that in both Ireland and Wales there are Churches for long established but now disestablished, in the latter case within living memory.

Nor even *within* the four countries which make up our geographical area has the situation been simple. It has possibly been closest to simplicity in Scotland, in which Presbyterianism is dominant. Even there, however, the divisions within that one confession have in the past brought great diversity of emphasis. In England, and to an even larger extent in Wales, the place of Churches which do not conform to the established Church has been a considerable one. The inter-play between the Church and Nonconformity has been a major influence upon the character of English life. To add yet another touch to our 'infinite variety' there is in Wales a great devotional tradition in another language than English.

The British ecclesiastical scene is not only of interest because of its variety within a compact area, but because of its originality. Of new forms of Christian churchmanship Britain has ever been a fecund mother. The great Anglican communion, now spread throughout the world by English settlement or missionary work, owes its origin, with all the religious development which has followed, to the break by the little island Church with the Pope. The world-wide fellowship of Methodist Churches, now considerably exceeding in its membership the confession from which it sprang, derives directly from the unwearying itinerant ministry of that man sent from God whose name was John Wesley. The smaller, but far from inconsiderable, body of Congregational Churches own an English origin. Smaller but still significant bodies found in many parts of the world also derive from British religious activity. The Quakers, or Society of Friends, wherever they are found, all look to George Fox, with his drastic rejection of all conventions that might mask unspirituality, as their founder under God. The far-flung work of the Salvation Army is in the most direct sense the product of William Booth's response in England to the call to succour the poor and desperate. Even the Disciples of Christ, known here as the Churches of Christ, while appearing to us to be a chiefly American form of churchmanship, owe the first impetus for their creation to Scottish evangelical piety.

It follows therefore, from the range and fertile character of British religious history, that a far from parochial interest attaches to it. Further, the fortunes in the contemporary world of Churches which have so clearly marked the religious development of the world may be held to concern all with a living interest in the cause of Christ's Church. It will be gratifying if a few readers of these pages are those who look upon the religious scene in Britain from elsewhere, and desire to understand it a little better.

It is probable, nevertheless, that the majority of readers will be themselves living within the religious life of one of the countries which form the British Isles. Can the necessarily brief and simple description of that life and history in the following chapters be other than a rather tedious description of things which are already known, affording only that strange pleasure given by local newspapers of reading accounts of events at which we have ourselves been present? A few years spent in trying to interpret the diversity of our religious situation up and down these islands suggests to me that this is not so. In fact most people know all too little of any Church other than their own, and our ignorance of the church life of the other three countries is often great. This small volume is therefore partly offered as a contribution to British ecumenical understanding. Only in relation to one Church—the Roman Catholic—is the tone, I hope, other than basically interpretative. Even the chapter about that Church is intended to be appreciative both of achievement and of those elements in her life which most forthrightly challenge other forms of churchmanship. But the sympathetic Roman Catholic reader himself must recognise that the dogmatic claims of his Church, and above all the 'un-churching' of everyone of different allegiance, compels a different treatment. I have sought to describe chiefly the present form and progress of the Roman Church here, rather than her dogma or ecclesiastical system.

Indeed, in regard to all the Churches here described little if any attempt has been made to set forth their doctrines or systems in any clear way. The treatment is deliberately existentialist, if a current 'cant' word may be permitted. One reason is that there are excellent books which give descriptions of doctrine, among which *Christendom*[1] by Einar Molland may be commended for its thoroughness. Another, and perhaps stronger, reason is that such necessarily brief accounts of a Church's faith and order as a short book can give often seem to bear as little resemblance to the actual life of the Church in question as a dusty stuffed pike may have to the living fish darting amidst the rushes. It may be easier to examine the stuffed fish, and indeed the living one may be so elusive as only to be glimpsed momentarily; but the stuffed fish is not really a fish at all.

It is recognised that this existentialist method is a bold one, since it too affords only glimpses and not the opportunity of seeing the Churches steadily and whole. Again, it runs the obvious dangers of being superficial and subjective. Yet again, it may seem almost absurdly concerned with what is going on in the Churches now, and what is their present state. For this I do not apologise. That is the book I have sought to write. The word 'today' in its title is taken seriously. Thus, I have not tried to give any full historical treatment to the Churches described in these pages, although they do of necessity contain a considerable amount of history. It is only such an amount as may help the reader to understand the Churches as they are today. It is that history which retains obvious present meaning. For example, it would be

[1] Published by Mowbrays, London, and Philosophical Library, New York.

impossible to understand the Church of England as it is to-day without some reference to the Tractarian Movement, or to grasp the problems besetting Protestant unity in Ireland without some reference to the chequered history of Anglican-Presbyterian relations there.

For the inaccuracies which must inevitably have crept into the attempt to cover so much within less than two hundred pages, I apologise in advance. Any distortions, moreover, of the position and life of any Church are as inadvertent as the errors of fact. The purpose has been to describe, and certainly not to misrepresent. Nevertheless the distinction between description and evaluation is a fine one in matters of this sort. A certain amount of comment has seemed admissible if the description were to be really focussed. Since the confession of other people's sins, normally known as gossip, is always more enjoyable than the confession of one's own, it has seemed good to ensure that such comment should be more free in regard to the English Free Churches, in whose heritage I stand, than in regard to any others.

Quotations from the poems of Mr John Betjeman on pp. 18 and 132 are by courtesy of the author and the publishers, Messrs John Murray Ltd.

1

THE CHURCH OF ENGLAND

'I have surveyed most Churches, Eastern and Western, in fifteen years ecclesiastical pilgrimage (during my voluntary banishment for my religion and loyalty), and I dare pronounce the Church of England what David said of Goliath's sword, "There is none like it:" both for Primitive Doctrine, Worship, Discipline and Government.'   *Isaac Basire* (1607-1676).

The Ideal of Comprehensiveness

ENGLAND is not overwhelmingly Anglican as Scotland is Presbyterian. The dissenting tradition, as we shall see, has exerted a strong formative influence upon English life. The village chapel, for all its aesthetic inadequacies, is part of the English scene as well as the more dominant parish church. Nevertheless no man could hope to understand England who did not study the English Church. It has always been suspicious of fanaticism, priding itself on tolerance and comprehension; but it has had a strange power to evoke a passionate love and loyalty such as are shown in the words of the Commonwealth exile whose words head this chapter. Even as mordant an observer of the English scene as George Orwell mentions as one of its characteristic fragments 'the old maids biking to Holy Communion through the mists of the autumn mornings'. If we think of an English village we picture an old church at the heart of it, surrounded by the graves of past generations, and in a wider circle the houses of the living. It would be mistaken to regard this as a symbol of the centrality of the Christian faith in our contemporary national life, but it rightly records the place that the Church has filled in our island story.

When the tourist wanders round an English cathedral or looks into the parish church, perhaps his chief impressions are of beauty and history. If so, the impressions are far from superficial. The Church of England immensely values both, and to recognise this is to have some clue to her particular character, and certainly to know the secret of her power to inspire love and devotion.

The Church of England is a product of the Reformation, and in brutal legal fact came into being as a result of an act of state. Henry VIII's determination to secure the Tudor succession by a male heir led to the break of the English Church with the Papacy and thus with the Western Church as it had existed for centuries. The poet Gray has sardonically referred to the time

> When love had taught a monarch to be wise,
> And gospel-light first dawn'd from Bullen's eyes.[1]

The same king's greed and astuteness led to the dissolution of the monasteries, which both filled the royal treasury and created a strong bulwark of vested interest against the restoration of the old ecclesiastical system. Those who received their share of the spoils did not want to see that page of history turned back.

Nothing, however, could be more absurd than to suggest that the English Church is the mere product of Tudor state-craft and the astute buying of support in the ranks of the up and coming new aristocracy. Henry's act was only possible because of the widespread ferment of Reformation ideas. There is little evidence that Henry had much sympathy with them, save in so far as he was a true Renaissance man, abundantly conscious of human abilities. He wanted to see as little change in the old religion as was compatible with his determination to be master of things ecclesiastical as well as political within his realm. But it was possible for him to

[1] Thomas Gray, *Alliance of Education and Government*, l. 108.

achieve his purposes because on religious grounds there was radical questioning of the claims of the Papacy and the form of the Western Church, as well as revulsion from its current corruption.

Thus the Church of England is quite plainly the result of the turbulent forces that broke the old unity of European Christendom. It is a reformed and Protestant Church in that sense, as it is a national Church in the sense of being legally created by the prince of the realm.

Nevertheless its wears its Protestantism with a difference, sufficient of a difference, indeed, as to make certain of its members hope that it will be mistaken for something else. Even the man who deprecates this minimising of the Anglican Protestant heritage must recognise the magnitude of the difference. Where John Calvin's thought guided the Reformation there came about a radical discontinuity with the mediaeval Church. The Church, as we shall see in a later chapter, was to be 're-formed' after the apostolic pattern, with a total rejection of the alleged accretions of succeeding centuries. There was, of course, a strong party in England who wanted to see the national reformation follow the pattern of that Lion of Geneva, John Calvin. The dominant and determining party willed otherwise. There was to be severance from the sovereignty of the Pope, and the abolition of abuses, notably as they centred on the monastic system. Apart from that there was to be the bare minimum of change. It can paradoxically be asserted that Henry VIII, who broke with the Papacy, also ensured the Catholic character of the Church of England. The emphasis of the English reformation came to be on the continuity with what had gone before rather than severance from it.

This is not a book in which the ensuing history of the Church of England can be traced, but two essential points must be made. The establishment of the Church was followed by a bewildering whirligig of change. The brief reign of Henry's son, Edward VI, marked the ascendancy of the party that desired a more thoroughgoing Protestant character for the Church. The succeeding reign of Mary Tudor (the Bloody Mary beloved of schoolboys who delight in excuse for the illicit epithet) marked the temporary power of those who rejected all reformation, and desired full submission to the power of Rome. These two violently contrasted successive chapters opened the way for the settlement in terms of comprehension which Elizabeth, who had inherited her father's astuteness, was determined to have. The Elizabethan settlement was a deliberate 'halting between two extremes'. Grim recent experience, as well as the national character, supported the will of the Queen. So also did the growing national feeling and patriotism of the age. There was determination to have a Church which took orders neither from Rome nor Geneva, but was the Church of the English people, with arms open enough to welcome all but the most stiff adherents of the old ways or most revolutionary proponents of the new. This ideal of national comprehension made a continuing mark upon the Church of England.

The other essential point which must be made from the succeeding history of the Church of England in its formative period is an entirely contrasted one. It is the *failure of the attempt at national comprehension*.

The failure was the product of Stuart obstinacy succeeded by Puritan rigidity. The Stuart successors of Elizabeth had neither her statecraft nor her wisdom. Charles I, in addition to his own defects of character, had that very un-Anglican figure, William Laud, as his Archbishop of Canterbury. He was un-Anglican not by being either Papist or Puritan, but in being unable to distinguish between sincerity and fanaticism. He was a truly Catholic Anglican of deep personal piety, yet he was also curiously akin to the contemporary Puritans who felt that men could be made moral and religious by legal enactment. It was into this error that the opposing party fell in the period of its power during the Common-wealth. The enmities which were created and nourished throughout the first sixty years of the seventeenth century shattered the comprehensiveness of the Church of England. The promulgation of the Clarendon Code with its penal provisions against those who dissented from the national Church finally broke the religious life of the nation into two. As Hensley Henson has said, 'Against the Puritan the Church's victory was Pyrrhic. The Church only overcame the Puritans at the cost of its religious monopoly, that is, of its national character.'[1]

These two elements, an ideal of comprehensiveness and its failure, continue to provide the paradox and tension of the life of the Church of England.

The Church's Continuity

When we look to what the Church of England preserved of the old once it was severed from papal supremacy, the sum is an impressive one. It preserved its buildings, the great cathedrals and the multitude of parish churches. The con-tinuity of physical structures can scarcely be exaggerated as an element in the Anglican sense of being part of the Catholic Church. After all, to the ordinary man the fact that he went to worship in the same building lessened the sense of change. The prayers might be different, after a time the priest might be differently vested and the altar ornaments changed, but it was the same building, the age-old centre of worship of the community. To the same ordinary man today the Anglican Church is *the* Church of England probably less because of her state relationship or her doctrinal claims, than because her buildings are rooted in the English landscape and full of the history of our people.

In the same way, the Church of England kept the con-tinuity of offices within the ministry. Here we think not only

[1] *The Church of England* (CUP), p. 17.

of the doctrinal claim to have preserved what that Church believes to be the three orders within the apostolic ministry, bishops, priests and deacons, though this is an element in it, but also of the maintenance of the continuity of particular offices, the line of Archbishops of Canterbury and of Vicars, say, of St Mary Redcliffe, Bristol. The structure of organisation as well as of buildings remained. The contrast with the reformation in Scotland, which was of the radical Calvinist type, is illuminating here. A great deal of the heritage of ancient buildings was lost, and the abolition of the hierarchy and the placing of ministers on a parity with one another in place of the priests and bishops of old changed the whole aspect of the Church. Changes there were, and of a drastic kind, in England but the preservation of outward forms has undoubtedly given to the Church of England something of its unique character as a reformed Church.

This leads us directly to the Anglican love of beauty. This must not be exaggerated. Not all our parish churches are Early English or Perpendicular gems, enriched by discovered Norman or Saxon arches. Many are of the nineteenth century, and some of these are spoilt by either parsimony or by ill-applied wealth. Almost all our churches have suffered from the hand of the restorer or the catalogue items of ecclesiastical furnishers. John Betjeman's hymn about the restoration of the church in 1883 enshrines a dominant aesthetic experience in many Anglican churches:

> Church furnishing! Church furnishing!
>   Sing art and crafty praise!
> He gave the brass for burnishing
>   He gave the thick red baize,
> He gave the new addition,
>   Pull'd down the dull old aisle,
> To pave the sweet transition
>   He gave th'encaustic tile.[1]

---

[1] *Selected Poems* (Murray), p. 127.

This, however, is but to say that zeal has often outrun both taste and historical sense. It remains true that the Church of England has had a sense of beauty, and that this has been related to her continuity with the past which she has treasured. The Puritan rejection of the pleasures of the senses can be exaggerated. The party that contained Milton and Marvell cannot be accused of total lack of interest in the arts. The Puritan nonetheless has always tended to suspicion that the created world may veil rather than reveal the Creator. With all the variety of ceremonial observance in the Church of England it cannot be said that any but a small party within Anglicanism have nourished that suspicion. Anglican buildings and worship have been marred by sloven- liness during periods of religious indifference, and by ex- cesses of restoring fervour or ritualistic imitation of foreign models at times of religious quickening. They have not been marred by fear of beauty.

We have written of those elements in the Church of Eng- land which stress her Catholicity and continuity. To describe that Church aright no less emphasis must be laid upon those changes which made her very different indeed from the Church of Rome. The original break—that from the authority of the Papacy—was a gigantic one. It meant not only a rejec- tion of a great deal of Roman doctrine, but embarkation upon a different line of development. We have spoken of the Church of England wearing its Protestantism with a dif- ference. It wears its Catholicity likewise. The Church of Rome and the Church of England are vastly different from one another to-day because of these many centuries of separate development.

The two dominant influences upon Anglican development have been the Bible and the Book of Common Prayer. The first is obviously not peculiar to Anglicanism, and the Puri- tans indeed protested that the Church of England was not truly reformed under the judgment of the Word of God. Be that as it may, the Church of England was in marked contrast with the Church of Rome in its use of the Bible. The translation of the Bible into the English tongue had been one of the creative forces in the English reformation; now the genius of Thomas Cranmer took the old liturgical forms and the new English Bible and produced the Book of Common Prayer. Stress must be laid upon the word 'Common'. Here again was a great departure from the Roman Church. The Prayer Book was in English, the vernacular. Almost miraculously, it was in English of glorious beauty. And the whole book was biblical through and through. The Church of England may without boasting claim to be in its worship the most biblical Church in Christendom. A devout Anglican who attends his eight o'clock Communion, Mattins and Evensong any Sunday will have sung several psalms and canticles of Scripture, and heard lections from a Gospel and an Epistle and four long readings, two from each Testament.

The Book of Common Prayer is certainly not beyond criticism. A few of its collects in their emphasis on rewards smack rather of Pharisaic Judaism than of the fulness of the Christian faith. The Order for the Burial of the Dead, for all its welcome realism in a day when we only 'pass on' or 'pass away' and never are allowed plainly to die, lacks to some the essential note of strong victory. At times, it has been suggested, the world of Tudor power politics finds reflection in its thought forms. These blemishes, if indeed they are there, remain superficial. It is the work of supreme religious genius, and one of the greatest of England's gifts to the world. It enshrines the Anglican spirit as nothing else does.

The Evangelicals and the Oxford Movement

Before we turn in the remainder of our chapter to some description of and comment upon the Church of England as it is today—which is our proper theme—two periods of her later history must be briefly mentioned. One is the period of Evangelical revival chiefly associated with the work of John Wesley, although with other tributary streams and a continuing flow after the main stream of the Methodist movement had become separated from the Church of England. John Wesley was an Anglican priest, and a deeply devoted one. Our following chapter deals a little more fully with that revival, but here it must be recognised that it was clearly meant by God to be a movement of renewal within the body of the Church of England, and that Methodism's development as a separate denomination marks the gravest distortion of the life of the English Church since the ideal of comprehension failed at the time of the Restoration.

This is seen more clearly when we consider the other movement of renewal which came through the work of the Tractarians, whose leaders were Newman, Keble and Pusey, from 1833 onwards. If the earlier movement was Evangelical, this might be described as 'churchly'. Discerning the signs of the times, the Tractarians, centred upon Oxford where most of them exercised their ministry, saw the danger of national apostasy from the Christian faith. (In this they may be deemed to have been truly prophetic.) They saw the tides of liberal, anti-clerical feeling rising on the Continent and only more slowly in Britain. The place of the Christian faith, and the Church which enshrined it, was being challenged in the ancient universities. The growth of new knowledge, and the coming of the industrialisation which was changing the pattern of England before men's eyes, were creating that secularism which dominates the minds of most men in developed societies today. William Nicholls has rightly said:

The Oxford Movement was before all else anti-liberal, and became Catholic as a means to that. Its association with the Romantic Movement led to the exaltation of the medieval or Gothic period as the model on which the contemporary life of the Church must be rebuilt.[1]

The Oxford Movement, or Tractarianism, was a revolt against the spirit of the age. It gave the impression of being conservative, reactionary and obscurantist. Indeed that was more than an impression. Its leaders believed that only in a return to the past, to the primitive doctrine of the Councils of the undivided Church, could the Church of England recover her ancient heritage and be seen in her true spiritual character. Thus, anything of reform, of toleration to dissenters and the like, imperilled the Ark of God. Above all the Tractarians were High Church, not in the popular sense of today, meaning ritualistic, but holding a high doctrine of the Church as no mere creature of the State but the Divine Society. It has always been a danger arising from Anglican origins that it should be Erastian; that is, that men should think of it as just the spiritual aspect of the State. This low view of the Church the Tractarians vehemently challenged. Unsympathetic though he was, Lytton Strachey summed up the point of contrast:

Other men saw in Christianity itself scarcely more than a convenient and respectable appendage to existence, by which a sound system of morals was inculcated, and through which one might hope to attain to everlasting bliss. To Newman and Keble it was otherwise. They saw a transcendant manifestation of Divine power, flowing down elaborate and immense through the ages; a consecrated priesthood, stretching back, through the mystic symbol of the laying on of hands, to the very Godhead; a whole universe of spiritual beings brought into communion with the Eternal by means of wafers; a great mass of metaphysical doctrines, at once incomprehensible and of incalculable import, laid

[1] In *Essays in Anglican Self-Criticism,* ed. David M. Paton (SCM Press), p. 24.

down with infinite certitude; they saw the supernatural everywhere and at all times, a living force, floating invisible in angels,
inspiring saints, and investing with miraculous properties the
commonest material things.[1]

Apart from one or two cheap touches this is deeply per-
ceptive. Supernatural, sacramental, divinely authoritative,
priestly and eternal—to the Tractarians the Church was all
these things. Admittedly, not a few, including Newman himself, finally discerned the lineaments of that Divine and
sacramental society in the Roman Church rather than in
that of their upbringing. Keble, Pusey and others stood firm.
It is their achievement, under God, to have utterly transformed the Church of England.

In almost every particular they were defeated, and sometimes their anxieties were pathetic to the point of the ludicrous. The ancient universities were transformed from
clerical preserves to lay societies, and their exclusively Anglican character was destroyed. The Irish Church was disestablished by state action. Roman Catholics and Dissenters
were increasingly emancipated from their remaining civil
disabilities. Biblical criticism became accepted as an essential
tool of Christian theology. Yet sober historical judgement
must be that no group of men has more completely altered
the succeeding history of their Church. (They would not have
relished the compliment, for they believed that they *appealed
to* the past—not only to the Early Fathers, but to the great
Anglican divines like Richard Hooker and Lancelot An-
drewes.) The Church of England today is what it is because
the Tractarians were what they were. The tragedy is that the
Church which nurtured within a century two of the world's
religious geniuses, John Wesley and John Henry Newman,
failed to hold either within her fold. Once again the ideal of
comprehensiveness failed. It is one of the fascinating ques-

[1] *Eminent Victorians* (Penguin), p. 25.

tions of history what would have been the later religious history of England if Newman's work had been done in a Church fertilised by the Methodist revival. Might there have been that synthesis between Evangelical and High Church principles which not even the hospitable arms of the English Church have been able to nourish?

It is piquant to realise that the Tractarian movement has been popularly accused of being the exact opposite of what it essentially was. Intensely conservative, it bore the outward appearance of a revolutionary march determined to challenge every accepted idea about the national Church. Almost anti-quarian in matters of liturgy and worship, it was constantly condemned for ruthless innovation. Utterly opposed to Dissent of every kind, it so disturbed the established Church as to drive not a few from fear of Popery into the Nonconformist Churches. Much of this arises not from the work of the first generation of the movement but from their successors. Men like Pusey and Keble were little, if at all, interested in outward ceremonial. The former had to have the nature of a cope explained to him late in his ministry, and to the end of his life celebrated from the north end of the altar (a mark today of strong Evangelical convictions). Their concern was with a doctrine of the Church, not with its ritual manifestations.

It is understandable that the next and succeeding generations should not be governed by this austere principle. There were several reasons for this. One was the effect on them of the Romantic Movement, as has been earlier suggested. The same forces which created a constituency for Sir Walter Scott and his romances of history sought in the recovery of the rich vestments, glowing windows, vaulted aisles and intoxicating incense of the Middle Ages fulfilment for emotions starved in the Age of Reason and unfulfilled by the steam locomotive and the factory.

Yet again, even for those who could see, however marred,

the lineaments of the true Catholic Church in the Church of England, there was strong temptation to borrow the ceremonial and usages which had been developed by the Church of Rome. Thus, despite the chilling attitude of the Supreme Pontiff to his separated Anglican brethren, they could feel themselves more fully a part, even if unrecognised, of the great Church of the West. The third reason was more honourable. 'It was largely,' says Dr J. R. H. Moorman, now Bishop of Ripon, 'with the object of attracting the poor of the great cities that the "ritualistic" movement began.' He is bound to add, however, that the ritualism was an almost logical development from the doctrine:

> It arose out of the theology of the Tractarians who had laid much emphasis on the Eucharist and on the doctrine of the Real Presence. This inevitably led to a desire not only for frequent celebrations of the Holy Communion but also to the wish to surround the altar with all that was bright and glorious, and to conduct the service with greater ceremonial.[1]

Unfortunately they ransacked Roman ritual to find what they sought, and so provided fuel for the flaming fears of the hidden hand of Rome. It was only much later that the research of Dr Percy Dearmer and others provided a ceremonial English in both its history and restraint.

Meanwhile the damage was done. Those who browse in Victorian history will recall the agitations about ritualism, the use of the arm of the law to restrain illegalities, the carrying off to gaol of heroic if misguided priests from Dockland parishes, the 'Roman fever' of emotional undergraduates, the excitement over sanctuary lamps, chasubles and the reservation of the Blessed Sacrament. It is a strange picture of mingled emotional fervour and concern about trivialities. Along with it went the fundamental Protestantism of the church-going classes (which were large), and the growing secularisation of both the intellectual and the working man.

[1] *A History of the Church in England* (A. & C. Black), p. 368.

To the English layman, irremediably Protestant, however enamoured of meaningless ritual in Masonry or the Ancient Order of Buffaloes, to be 'High Church' was to be pseudo-papist, ritualistic and even effeminate.

It is lamentable that this should still be the picture of the High Church movement in the minds of many English Free Churchmen and members of the Church of Scotland. Partly this comes from using externals as the basis of judgment. Vestments are unjustifiably associated with Romanism. More seriously, since the Tractarian position is founded upon the conception of the Church possessing a ministry coming down in unbroken succession from the apostles, it has certainly led to a great rigidity of attitude to non-episcopal communions. This is understandably resented. It is still to be regretted that these same communions have not sufficiently recognised that the same classically 'high' doctrine of the Church as, in several ways, brought them into being, is, in a very different mode, enshrined in the Tractarian movement. If Anglicans had no better doctrine of the Church than that of the spiritual aspect of the State, it would be hard indeed for Presbyterian or Congregationalist, Baptist or Methodist, to find any 'universe of discourse' with them. The fact is that, vastly divided as they still are as to the marks of the Divine Society, since the work of the Oxford Movement Anglicans are one with their non-episcopal brethren in believing of the Church that

> She is His new creation,
> By water and the word.

Church and State Today

As we examine therefore the Church of England to-day we find a Church in which that movement of 'churchly' renewal has done its work. Its priests and faithful communicants have no doubt that they are part of the whole Catholic Church.

It remains nevertheless a national Church. It is not the Church of the English nation. Since the Test and Corporation Acts it has certainly not been the spiritual home even of the religious portion of the nation. Although the great mass of children are still baptised at her fonts, the Church of England is little more than 'the Church they stay away from' to those who, in the forces or in hospital, would register themselves as 'C. of E.' It is national in two ways—in origin and in particular relationship. The Church of England is now the mother Church of a great world-wide communion. It has, however, all sprung from the settlement or missionary work of members of the Church of England or, less directly, from her daughter Churches. This is an amazing story of the expansion of a Church which vanished from the map of Christendom during the period of the Commonwealth.

Today the particular relationship of the Church of England to the nation survives despite the abandonment of religious observance by the greater part of the community. It still possesses immense privileges. The monarch, who must be a member of the Church of England, is crowned by the Archbishop of Canterbury, who sits in the House of Lords, with his brother of York and twenty-four other bishops. The overwhelming majority of ceremonial occasions in national and civic life are religiously in the hands of that Church.

For all this a price is exacted. The Church of England is not free to choose her leaders. Bishops and Deans are nominated by the Crown on the advice of the Prime Minister of the day. He may not be an Anglican, or even a Christian believer. Although increasingly he may act on ecclesiastical advice, the right rests with him and with nobody else. The final decision in church law rests with the Judicial Committee of the Privy Council. Her worship is in the last resort subject to the decisions of Houses of Parliament composed of members of every religious persuasion and of none. This last point is no oddity of obsolete law. The only thorough-going attempts to revise the Book of Common Prayer to make it more consonant with contemporary religious needs and ecclesiastical practice were defeated in the House of Commons in 1927 and 1928—in the first case chiefly by an emotional 'No Popery' speech by a Scottish Presbyterian. Although there are few in the Church of England, or indeed outside it, who desire disestablishment of the Church, there are many who yearn to see a form of national recognition of religion which yet, after the model of the Church of Scotland, grants spiritual autonomy. It will not be easy to achieve, nor should it be forgotten that the Scottish freedom was obtained with a great price.

There is certainly no agitation among the English Free Churches for the disestablishment of the Church of England, whatever residual resentments there may be about her privileges. This was made plain in a report presented to the Free Church Federal Council in 1953 by the Commission on Church and State that it had appointed three years earlier. This report, *The Free Churches and the State,* had a temperate tone which would have gravely shocked the Liberation Society which toiled in earlier decades with vehement Free Church support to secure both the disestablishment and disendowment of the Church of England. But there are agitations possible only in a time of general religious prosperity. Before the flood of secularism a more brotherly feeling obtains. When the ship is holed sailors do not spend the time complaining that the captain has a better fitted cabin than they enjoy.

The Bishop and the Diocese

How is this national Church organised? There are two provinces, Canterbury and York, which contain, very unequally divided, forty-three dioceses and over eleven and a half thousand parishes. The Church of England is in organisation essentially both episcopal and parochial. The bishop of the diocese is the key figure in the wider church life. The parish is the basic unit in local church life. To use the word 'organisation' is itself misleading, unless it be recognised that the organisation is for pastoral purposes. In the words of the late Archbishop Garbett, 'The diocese is not to be to him (the bishop) a large administrative machine which he must control, but a fellowship of parishes, the clergy and laity of which he must do his utmost to shepherd.'[1]

Upon the bishop rests immense responsibility. He has the final right to decide whom he will ordain to the holy ministry. In recent years the recruitment of the ministry and the testing of vocation have been far more systematically, and much more centrally, discharged through the Central Advisory Council for the Ministry and its predecessor. Still the final decision on admission rests with the bishop, and it is his hands which are laid upon the ordinand to make him successively deacon and priest. (There is usually a year's interval between these acts.) The bishop is the father in God to the diocese, and has a special pastoral relationship to the clergy. He is the *pastor pastorum*.[2] He is also responsible for their moral discipline.

The most intimate way in which the bishop represents the wider Church to the laity is through his ministration of the rite of confirmation. In a large diocese the confirmations impose a heavy burden of work upon the bishop. He must nevertheless rejoice, if he be a man of truly pastoral heart, that in the midst of multifarious administrative cares he is so constantly enabled to lay his hands upon and address boys and girls offering themselves to 'the young Prince of Glory'. Leaving aside for the moment all doctrinal questions of the place of episcopal confirmation, it is plain that the bishop's presence and act vividly represent the entrance of the person

[1] *The Claims of the Church of England* (Hodder & Stoughton), p. 97.
[2] Pastor of pastors.

confirmed into the fellowship of the whole Church. What remains strange to non-Anglican churchmen is the absence of any balancing emphasis upon entrance into membership of, and responsibilities in, a particular congregation. An Anglican writer, speaking however from the experience of the Church of South India, has recently written:

> It appears to be possible to be baptised, confirmed and a communicant member of the Church of England without ever accepting the responsibilities and privileges of membership of any particular congregation. That is I believe a dangerous error.[1]

In addition, however, to these and many other pastoral responsibilities and opportunities the bishop is the very heart of what must of necessity be a considerable administrative machine. He also has considerable demands laid upon his time by the wider work of the Church, in Convocation, Church Assembly and its councils and committees, and—in many cases—in ecumenical bodies. Yet again, if he be in one of the pre-eminent sees, Canterbury, York, London, Durham and Winchester, or among the twenty-one most senior other bishops, he will have a seat in the House of Lords. The modern bishop, whatever his faults, is no lotus eater.

What may be more in question is whether he can truly be a father in God. Considerable controversy has raged throughout this century on the size of dioceses. Many new ones have been created in the last hundred years, although the increase in population has been proportionately much greater. There remain almost fantastic variations in the size of dioceses, ranging from Hereford, with a population of 220,000 and some two hundred and fifty parochial clergy, to London with four million in population and almost eight hundred clergy. Even historical reasons can scarcely defend such disproportion. Smaller dioceses can bring problems, notably in the difficulty of facilitating the movement of clergy from heavier to lighter duties. Certainly the multiplying of bishops reduces

[1] A. M. Hollis in *Essays in Anglican Self-Criticism*, p. 217.

the impression of the bishop being an important 'national officer', to use a phrase beloved by the late Bishop Hensley Henson. It may be doubted, in any case, whether this is a very spiritual conception, save in so far as the comparative rarity of the diocesan bishop gives weight to his public utterances and therefore enables him to catch the ear of the public with a Christian word. This function of the episcopate may well be judged to be a wasting asset.

The Parson and the Parish

If the bishop and the diocesan unit have been much discussed, so also has the local unit—the parish. The attribution of the parish system to St. Theodore of Tarsus, Archbishop of Canterbury 668-690, is apocryphal, but the system has remained virtually unchanged since Anglo-Saxon times, save for the necessary breaking up of many large parishes as the population of towns and cities has so vastly grown. At the heart of the parish is the rector or vicar. The ideal of the ministry of the Church of England is the faithful parish priest in the midst of his flock. Its most clear literary expression is probably found in George Herbert's *The Country Parson*. Of course it has been an ideal constantly unrealised. Readers of Jane Austen will recall the normal picture of the parson as a lesser squire living a life of leisure. Readers of harsher portraits will remember how often the incumbent was an absentee, sometimes from a number of livings held in plurality, and the curate who did the work was ill-educated and desperately poor. There remains, nonetheless, a certain continuity of pastoral care in the English village. Those who have discovered the delights of the diary of Parson Woodforde (1758-1802) will recognise that even before the quickening of Evangelical or Tractarian revival there were honest parsons who cared for their flocks. Certainly with the coming of those revivals the standard of clerical duty was transformed. Indeed, it may be wondered whether the whole Church of England does not suffer at the present time from the notion that clerical activity of the comparatively short Victorian period is the norm of pastoral practice.

That activity was based on two things—the economic prosperity of a period of religious 'boom', and the parallel provision of an abundant supply of cheap curates. The first provided the parsonage with ready domestic labour; the latter enabled the parish to be 'worked'. Maidservants have disappeared, and curates are disappearing. Not the least disturbing feature of contemporary church life to-day is the pathetic pretence that the Victorian pattern of the parish can be maintained despite these facts. It cannot, and there appears little reason for the deification of that period.

The effect of the shortage of clergy on the parish system is dramatic. It is estimated that in 1901 there were some 23,670 clergy in the provinces of Canterbury and York. In 1921 there were still 22,579. In 1951 there were only 18,196. Even more striking is the fact that today there are 3,263 persons to every clergyman below the age of 65. In 1901 there were only 1,570.

To this it may be rejoined that the demand for their services is much less and that therefore the increased number of people to be ministered to is merely notional. But this is to cut at the roots of the most spiritual claim which the Church of England has to be called national. This is the parochial system, and the inalienable right of the parishioner to be cared for by the parson of the parish. Once admit that the parson has really only the care of those who seek his services and the national claim of the Church of England would become ludicrous.

How then can the parochial system be maintained? For in addition to the shortage of clergy there must also be noted the rightful use of clergy for specialised ministries, such as in industry or in universities. Such specialisms are in effect an application of the parochial principle, the seeking of people where they are to be found. But they reduce still further the number available for the basic parish ministry. One big adjustment has been in the grouping of rural parishes. This has often led to resentments. A man resident in another village is not 'our vicar' in the old sense, and the necessity for a monthly pattern of changing service times seems to place unendurable strains on the memory of would-be worshippers. The arrangement certainly imposes a heavy burden of Sunday duty upon the incumbent, but it can hardly be claimed that he has an impossible pastoral task if he has reasonable transport.

Far more difficult to solve is the densely populated urban parish, where a vicar and curate, the latter possibly only in deacon's orders, may be set to minister to some twenty thousand people. A Presbyterian author may be permitted to say that the faithful incumbent of such a parish—and the standard of duty is impressively high—is among the most hardworked men in the country today. The preparation for and conduct of worship, the interviews with those seeking baptism for their children or marriage for themselves, the visiting of the sick and aged, the taking of funerals and the comforting of the bereaved, together with the essential or- ganisation of youth work and so forth absorb almost every hour of the working day. The maintenance of personal devotional life, let alone the seeking of refreshment of mind and spirit in reading of a deeper sort, must demand great discipline. How in addition can the parish be 'worked' in the old sense? The plain answer is that it cannot. The door-to- door visitation which was the mainstay of the well-worked Victorian parish is impossible in the urban parish, save when it is exceptionally well-staffed.

Where the parson is resolute that the parish must be cared for he is being forced into a new and vitalising apprehension of the Church. The Church of England has always been tempted towards an unduly clerical conception of the Church of God. Popular phrases such as 'he is thinking of entering the Church', used of the potential ordination candidate, are not insignificant. The Church of England has never used the laity as have the Church of Scotland and the Free Churches. To-day, partly under the pressure of pastoral necessity, the Church of England is rediscovering her laity. In many a town parish and new housing estate the committed laity are acting as 'street wardens', representing the Church in their road, making known to the clergy where there is greatest need for their pastoral ministry, and letting it be seen that the Church cares. A good deal of steady visitation is being done by the laity. A watch is kept for the arrival of the removal van and the Church welcomes new parishioners through the street warden and then through the parson.

This rediscovery of the laity must go far beyond learning the layman's usefulness in the Church. Our present concern, however, is with the layman as pastor. This use of the laity does not preclude the need for more clergy; but neither must it be seen as providing merely an *ersatz* working of the parish. It may be exceedingly salutary that God's people cannot readily hire a supply of curates to carry out their duties to care for their neighbours and win them for the flock of Christ. It would certainly be odd if just when the Free Churches are coming to recognise a parochial responsibility, the Church of England were to abrogate her age-old responsibility. One Archbishop, Dr Joost de Blank of Cape Town, has confessed that he became an Anglican just because of the inescapable responsibility that the Church of England recognised for everyone within the parish. In the intensely missionary situation in which the Church finds itself today the parochial system must not be seen as an irrelevant relic of a past Christian era. It is, rather, a salutary reminder of the commitment of the Church to the winning of the world outside as well as to the nourishing of its own inner life.

Spiritual Life

The power of the Church of England to exercise an evan-gelistic parochial ministry will nevertheless depend chiefly upon her inner life. What is the character of the worshipping devotional life of that Church? It is, of course, intensely varied. We have ourselves experienced an area where two contiguous parish churches were so contrasted that in one case the Communion office was said in Latin between the English words, and in the other the Holy Table and its sur-roundings were entirely bare save for a large brass offertory plate ('Perpetual reservation of the alms dish', as a Catholic-minded friend wickedly described it.) It is still true that these extremes are exceptional, and that there is a central tradition and development in Anglican worship that belongs neither to Father Hugh Chantry-Pigg or his zealous opponents, the 'Protestant storm-troopers', in Rose Macaulay's delightful guide to Anglican diversity, *The Towers of Trebizond*.

At the heart of that development is the centrality of the Holy Communion. During the Victorian era attendance at Morning or Evening Prayer was the norm. 'Many people,' states J. R. H. Moorman, 'followed the example of Queen Victoria and the Prince Consort in receiving the Holy Com-munion only twice a year.'[1] In the eighteenth century provision in most parishes for receiving the Sacrament was rare. It was the work of the Tractarians to make a weekly celebration normal in every parish church. Celebrations on weekdays are common, and in churches of strongly Catholic tradition a daily celebration is the rule.

In recent decades the Communion has become yet more central in a growing number of churches. The effect of the celebration at 8 o'clock in the morning, without music, when contrasted with the well attended sung Mattins and Even-song at 11 and 6.30, was a subtle suggestion that it was the

[1] *Op. cit.*, p. 390.

less central service, to be attended perhaps monthly. Now in a growing number of parishes the Holy Communion, or Eucharist, is made quite plainly the main act of worship of the Lord's Day. It is usually at some such hour as 9.30, and is often followed by a simple parish breakfast, an invaluable occasion of fellowship. It is to this Family Eucharist that the main body of the worshipping faithful are expected to come. It is not the same as the 11 o'clock Sung Mass which many Catholic-minded churches used to have, with elaborate ceremonial and a minimal number of communicants. This is the Christian family coming together at God's Board. The service will be sung and the word will be preached, albeit briefly, usually from the Gospel for the day.[1]

There have doubtless been losses in the dethroning in many parishes of the service of Morning Prayer. These have been aggravated by the great diminution of attendance at evening worship which has been experienced recently by Churches of almost every tradition. The Old Testament is rarely read in the Communion; although experiments are in places being made by adding a third lection to the traditional Gospel and Epistle. The sermon, by pressure of time, is often reduced to a short homily, and sustained teaching and solid expository preaching are little heard. The Archbishop of Canterbury, Dr Ramsey, while welcoming the new developments for their positive contribution sounds a cautionary note:

> I believe also that there is still much to be learnt from the Matins and Sermon whereby congregations were nurtured in the Scriptures. May we never have a generation of worshippers unfamiliar with the Canticles and the Psalms! ... Above all, there was, and

[1] It is one of the odder anomalies of a Church not markedly deprived of them that for long enough it was the custom not to have a sermon at the one service where the Book of Common Prayer prescribes one, and always to have one on Sunday at Morning and Evening Prayer when there is no suggestion of one in the set service.

is, much to be learnt from the quiet, early celebration. It keeps
alive, and gives real place to, the *meditative* element in religion.
It is the meditative element which is desperately needed, and so
often imperilled.[1]

One way in which a small but growing number of Anglicans has sought to deepen that meditative element has been
through the making of a retreat. Many dioceses are now
possessed of centres for retreats, and they have undoubtedly
been spiritual power-houses. They represent one more fruit
of the Tractarian movement in the Church of England.

Yet another fruit which has greatly affected the Church at
many points is the restoration of the religious orders. It is
difficult indeed to picture the Church of England today
without them. The Society of the Sacred Mission at Kelham,
founded by Father Herbert Kelly, a classic Anglican
'original', and the Community of the Resurrection at Mirfield, founded by Bishop Charles Gore, have played a large
part in widening the background of recruitment for the priesthood. Mirfield men, like Bishop Trevor Huddleston and
Father Hugh Bishop, CR, have become widely influential
Christian apologists. The Society of St John the Evangelist
at Cowley, Oxford, is particularly active in parochial missions. The Anglican Franciscans toil today in unpromising
situations like Cable Street in Stepney, in ways that would be
dear to the heart of St Francis. Direct ways of service such
as these are the more obvious manifestations of the life of
the men's orders, and of those for women which have been
developed as fully; but their chief work is one of prayer. The
whole witness of the religious orders is a standing challenge
to the values of the present age. The vows to poverty, chastity
and obedience are to the very opposites of the materialism,
sensuality and license which are commonly exalted among us.

[1] *Durham Essays and Addresses* (SPCK), pp. 20-21.

Anglicans and Other Churches

The work of the Tractarians, in addition to shaping so much of the life and worship of the Church of England itself, has also much affected its relationship with other Churches. By its very character it gave the Church of England a greater concern for better relations with the great Church of the West. Intermittent conversations took place from 1921-1926 between certain Anglican leaders and such ecumenically-minded Roman Catholics as Cardinal Mercier and the Abbé Portal. These Malines Conversations did not end as abruptly as similar ones thirty years earlier, which were broken off by the Pope's brusque condemnation of Anglican orders, but died rather of sheer inanition. The unremitting obduracy of Rome was perhaps one factor in the considerable attention that has been given during this century to fellowship with the Orthodox and Eastern Churches. These Churches, with the break-up of the long reign of the Ottoman Empire, had begun to emerge into the western world. If the Pope proved unwelcoming, surely Orthodoxy, itself not in communion with Rome but claiming as direct descent from the great Oecumenical Councils of the undivided Church, would see in the Church of England a sister Church? The declaration of the Oecumenical Patriarch on Anglican orders was certainly far more forthcoming than that of the Pope, and warm relations have grown up in a number of ways. Those relations have nonetheless stopped short of intercommunion.

The enrichment which this fellowship with the Orthodox Churches has brought has been real. One does not look to such Churches with their long experience of suppression and restriction for greater light upon the prophetic function of the Church. But the very restriction had forced those Churches to seek that life which is hid with Christ in God. Here too was an invaluable corrective to the notion that only in Roman practice and devotion was any fount of Catholic renewal to be found. The Roman tradition was legal, with its emphasis on defined creed and dogma. The Orthodox tradition was supremely 'doxological'. The offering of praise and adoration through the Liturgy was the chief work of the Church. Anglicanism has been indubitably enriched by its contact with an age-old Christian tradition completely different from the activist one which makes its most ready appeal to the English temperament.

While closer relations with Rome on any terms save full submission to Papal claims were utterly remote, it was unrealistic to attach too much importance to friendly relations with Churches geographically distant from the place where the Church of England's main mission and ministry must be performed. The real crux for England is the relationship between the established Church and the Free Churches. Could the ideal of a truly national and comprehensive Church, which has been the never-abandoned Anglican dream, find fulfilment in the twentieth century? Here the Tractarian influence is more ambivalent. It has made the Church of England believe in a true and visible unity in a way that is far from universal among Free Churchmen. It has at the same time made that visible unity infinitely more difficult to secure.

David Edwards has summed up the Anglican position today in this regard in this way:

> To Anglicans, it is not enough to have spiritual unity if this is not expressed in sacramental fellowship; and it is not right to have sacramental fellowship, save in exceptional circumstances, unless there is a substantial measure of agreement in doctrine and of submission to a common spiritual authority. Anglicans reject the idea that co-operation, or federation, is all that is required of divided Churches.[1]

The emphasis of the Church of England on visible unity has been a valuable one. Its rejection of mere federation,

[1] *Not Angels but Anglicans* (SCM Press), p. 113.

which Bishop Lesslie Newbigin has stigmatised as 'reunion without repentance', is as valuable. The stumbling-block up to now has been what Anglicans have seen as the essential prerequisites of the achievement of visible unity. They have made the Anglican communion the most isolated in the world, possessing intercommunion only with the tiny Old Catholic Church and the (Lutheran) Church of Sweden. Even in regard to the last-named of these, some strain is being experienced at the present time as a result of its ordination of women to the priesthood.

The prerequisites for Anglicans of the achievement of visible unity are set out in their classic form in the Lambeth Quadrilateral, originally enunciated by the Lambeth Conference of 1884, but memorably enshrined in revised form in the 'Appeal to All Christian People' made by the later Conference of 1920. With three of the four points comparatively little difficulty is experienced by non-episcopal Churches. They are: (1) 'The Holy Scriptures as the record of God's revelation of Himself to man, and as being the rule and ultimate standard of faith'; (2) the Nicene and Apostles' Creeds; and (3) the sacraments of Baptism and Holy Communion. The rub has always come with the fourth point: 'A ministry acknowledged by every part of the Church as possessing not only the inward call of the Spirit but also the commission of Christ and the authority of the whole body.' The actual words of this point of the Quadrilateral of themselves provide no stumbling-block. Their consistent interpretation by Anglicans[1] to mean a ministry ordained by bishops standing in the historic or apostolic succession has proved until now the insuperable barrier to any union in these islands of Anglican and Free Churches.

[1] In fairness it must be stated that the 1888 version of the fourth point reads: 'The Historic Episcopate, locally adapted in the methods of its administration to the varying needs of the nations and peoples called of God into the Unity of His Church'. The more eirenical phrasing of 1920 was well-intentioned, but misleading.

While there is widely varying belief in the Church of England about the meaning of episcopacy—a diversity which has found expression in a good deal of recent writing on the subject—there is almost a complete agreement that it must be at the heart of any re-united Church. Naturally this conviction is held by those who are most fully heir to the Tractarian position, and believe that the bishop is the literally indispensable channel of grace through ordination. But it is also held by many who would not by any means go as far as that. They see in the bishop a symbol of the continuity and unity of the Church, and without wanting to define too precisely God's way of being gracious to his Church through the bishop, yet feel the office to be a precious gift to the Body of Christ, most zealously to be preserved. That feeling, quite apart from any doctrine of episcopacy, is a very real part of Anglican consciousness today.

How Strong is the Church?

We have left to the end of our chapter any assessment of the condition of the Church of England today, having deliberately devoted most of our space to a description of her ethos and the character of her religious life. The symposium *Essays in Anglican Self-Criticism,* which we have already cited, quotes an astringent criticism from outside that is at least provocative. It comes from Angus Wilson, the novelist:

> Despite a certain contemporary intellectual adherence...; despite a certain upper-middle-class return to church attendance as a defence against post-war social change; despite the periodic, somewhat nauseating religious exhortations of the popular press; the Church of England remains, I should think, in a steady decline.[1]

That there has been 'a certain contemporary intellectual adherence' even this hostile critic is bound to acknowledge. Mr T. S. Eliot, if by far the greatest, is by no means the only

Op. cit., p. 222.

considerable contemporary poet to find a satisfying spiritual home in Anglicanism. In a writer like C. S. Lewis Anglicanism, and indeed the whole Christian cause, has gained an apologist such as earlier only Romanism possessed in Chesterton and Belloc. It has never been the way of the Church of England to parade her 'scalps at the cassock belt', but acquaintance with any university will reveal many quietly faithful communicants among its senior members, many of whom have come to faith in maturer years.

We may be more doubtful of the return of the upper-middle-class even as a fact, let alone of the dubious motive somewhat arbitrarily provided to account for it. Our dubiety extends to the connection of the religious exhortations of the popular press (infrequent enough not only to have failed to induce nausea but even to attract our attention) with the poor Church of England. Where the Church of England has gained vast publicity has been in the televising of royal religious occasions, such as the Coronation or the wedding of the Princess Elizabeth and the Princess Margaret; but it is singularly difficult to assess the real religious impact of the Church's part at such times. That the Church is seen there as providing worship of amazing order and beauty is true. Whether it makes any real connection with the viewers' own spiritual needs is more questionable.

But is Angus Wilson's main, devastating judgment true—that the Church of England remains in steady decline? The evidence, such as it is, does suggest some numerical decline in Easter communicants.[1] Nevertheless, to jump from that figure to any assertion that the Church of England as such is in steady decline would be unjustified. The very character of the figure may relate more to the nominal than to the real in church loyalty.

[1] At Easter in 1956, 2,348,354 persons communicated in English parish churches. In 1958 the figure had fallen to 2,246,166, a 5% decrease.

What of the Church of England's leadership? Constant comparison is made with the days of great personalities on the episcopal bench like Henson and Gore; but, if it had not been for his (humanly speaking) untimely death, William Temple might have been Archbishop of Canterbury until five or six years ago, and Cyril Garbett, Archbishop of York, died but that time past. Temple was one of the great men of world history and Garbett must by any reckoning be accounted a great Anglican. We deliberately refrain from speaking of those now living, a practice which ecclesiastical writers too readily learn from the columnist. If in younger men it is impossible to see a Temple, that is hardly surprising. He was a gift the whole Church of God could not expect to receive twice in a century. Nor can the Church necessarily expect to have as many of the front rank leaders of the country as in a day when the opportunities for serving one's fellow men were more narrowly restricted. But we would judge that there are among the younger men in the Church of England potential leaders of quite significant power.

And if among the rank and file of the clergy there are not a few who have lost heart, lacking the stimulus of wider response, and denied any share in the affluent society about them, there are certainly a far greater number who gladly b.ace themselves for just the kind of challenge which a day such as this presents. There is more varied and vigorous experiment in ways of making the Church's mission effective in the Church of England than in any other British Church. It may still be doubted whether such experiments are making any marked impression upon those wholly outside the range of the Church's life; but a Church as fertile in such consecrated ingenuity is hardly upon its death-bed.

The greatly increased efficiency of the Church of England may obviously be variously interpreted. There are those who see in it an obsession with machinery which tries to disguise deep failure in fulfilling the Church's real task. Certainly the devising of machinery is no substitute for clarity and conviction in evangelism and faithfulness in pastoral care. But it is as certainly an unspiritual illusion that God asks us to be inefficient. In recent years, under the leadership of Dr Fisher as Archbishop of Canterbury, there has been a thoroughgoing attempt to put the Church's house in order.

It was after the First World War that, as a result of the Life and Liberty movement, in which William Temple played a pre-eminent part, the national Church Assembly was set up. This provided the Church with its own parliament which could initiate legislative action subject only to Parliamentary veto. Not only did that Assembly deliver the Church from the necessity of promoting a bill in Parliament through the normal channels for every essential adjustment in her life, but it also brought the laity for the first time into the conciliar government of the Church. Previously there had only been the Convocations, wholly clerical bodies which meet in the two provinces of Canterbury and York, each possessing two houses, of bishops and clergy. The Church Assembly is to all intents and purposes the Convocations with a house of laity added. The Convocations, which are of greater antiquity than Parliament, continue to meet, and doctrinal decisions are reserved to them. (Thus, for example, the laity had no voice whatever in determining the attitude of the Church of England to the Church of South India.)

The Church Assembly has disappointed those who, like Dick Sheppard, yearned for a revolution within the Church, but it has opened the way to the great present increase in the Church's efficiency and potential strategic deployment of her resources. The Church Commissioners have set in order a great deal of the historic material heritage of the Church. A vast policy of re-investment has increased her revenues and made them less inadequate for the many demands laid upon a Church committed to a nation-wide ministry. That policy has not been without its critics, for not a few see danger in making the Church too directly dependent upon the existing commercial and industrial order; but certainly it has cushioned the Church of England against the impact of inflation as no other Church has been protected.

With this more remunerative use of the generosity of past generations has gone in very recent years a vigorous policy of teaching Christian stewardship of resources. Already in many parishes it has transformed the situation. For the first time parishioners have been awakened to the duty and joy of maintaining God's work properly, and there has been deliverance from the sordid artifices with which the Church has been kept at a level of half-efficiency for far too long. What the Free Churches have of necessity long known is being discovered by the Church of England with great profit; that those who give properly to their Church become more deeply committed to it.[1]

Such movements as Christian stewardship have also a unifying influence in a Church that has been much divided by party allegiance. We may agree with A. M. Allchin when he says that 'the old extremes of party conflict within Anglicanism are over; the parties as we have known them in the past are in fact dead, even if some are still lingering over the funeral ceremonies'.[2] This is partly due to the situation which challenges the whole Church. There is something worse than unseemly in the uttering of the parrot-cries of theological and ecclesiastical party when men seem unable to hear the word of the Gospel itself with conviction. But

[1] In view of the common notion that the Church of England is maintained by the State, it is perhaps worth noting that of the £17½m. income of Parochial Church Councils in 1956, no less than £11½m. came from ordinary contributions. Endowments, legacies and special appeals account for the remainder. Even with the skilful reinvestment of the ancient patrimony of the Church by the Church Commissioners, it seems probable that the proportion contributed directly by congregations will grow. Christian Steward-ship campaigns are likely to ensure this.

[2] *Essays in Anglican Self-criticism,* p. 177.

there have been also many factors which have drawn the parties together. The abandonment by all but a tiny fringe of Anglo-Catholics of the facile imitation of Roman usages in worship, and the corresponding forsaking by many Evangelicals of the more obdurate objections to particular liturgical practices, have greatly helped. Both parties have come to have a greater love of both beauty and restraint in worship. In a much earlier period, 'Protestant vigilance was easily alarmed, but even an Ulsterman could hardly suspect that the hand of the Pope was at work when the Communion Table ceased to be a depository for hats, the font a receptacle for umbrellas.'[1] The process has gone on and Evangelicals today would accept practices which a generation ago would have been spurned as Anglo-Catholic. On the other side, the influence of such movements as 'Parish and People', with their strong stress upon the participation of the whole congregation in the Eucharist, and thus against the offering of the Mass as a holy spectacle, have worked a transformation of many churches with a firm Catholic teaching. That many individual instances can be adduced to contradict both these suggestions we do not doubt. There are Anglo-Catholic churches whose worship seems to have but tenuous connection with the Book of Common Prayer, and Evangelical ones which preserve an ungainly austerity in the ornaments and conduct of worship. But the coming together is marked.

Not the least contributory factor is the greater vitality of the Evangelical wing of the Church. From a period when it was entirely over-shadowed by the vigour of the Catholic revival it has now entered a time of recovery, and is able to make a contribution to a more balanced Church through the quality of its leadership and scholarship. (We do not refer to the disturbing recent increase in the number of ordinands from certain strongly 'party' theological colleges who mani-

[1] G. M. Young, *Victorian England: Portrait of an Age* (OUP), p. 73.

fest one aspect of the strange contemporary recrudescence of fundamentalism. Their effect upon the Church has yet to be seen.) There are those with strong and positive Evangelical convictions, but appreciation of others' churchmanship, who correct the ever present danger in the Catholic mind of a churchly Pelagianism.[1] There is a great Evangelical tradition in the Church of England with a glorious record both in oversea missionary activity and in social reform in this country. But for far too long those who stood in that tradition had retreated from concern with the life of the Church, and exclusively concerned themselves with the salvation of individuals. Their witness therefore went by default in the councils and committees of the Church. It is wholly to the good that that day is over, and there is a vigorous participation by Evangelicals in diverse aspects of the Church's life. It cannot but help to make the Church of England tread more clearly that *via media* which has been her true ideal.

That ideal of 'the middle way' has been, like all ideals, most imperfectly realised in history. The hope of comprehension has never been fulfilled, and her yearning to gather her separated chickens under her wing has often seemed to be limited to the offer of that refuge without any willingness to be bestirred to gather them. Even the valiant effort of the Archbishop of Canterbury in his famous Cambridge Sermon in 1946 to break through the barriers between established and Free Churches called on the latter to do something rather than announced action by the former. But, strong though the influence of the Free Churches has been upon our history, the Church of England could exercise a leadership both in unity and mission which would be readily acknowledged by the great majority of English Christians. Never in its history has that Church been so free from abuses, so unentangled in

[1] A deliciously unconscious example of this is to be found in the Bishop of Ripon's observation, 'John Newton (1725-1807) was one of the few Evangelicals who could preach about sin from close personal experience'! *A History of the Church in England,* p. 306.

its spiritual life with worldly interests. If there are no signs of revival in the sense of a gathering in of men in significant numbers from the world outside, there are definite marks both of inward renewal, and willingness to face deeper encounter with the world in mission. It may be that a far more drastic adjustment of her ways may have to be faced before that mission can be properly undertaken in a world fantastically altered by both scientific and social revolution. The Preface to the Book of Common Prayer realistically says, 'There was never anything by the wit of man so devised, or so sure established, which in continuance of time hath not been corrupted.' The Church of England has dealt manfully with the corruption, but the same 'continuance of time' brings also the demand for change. The test of the coming years will be of whether she can walk, in other well-known words of the Preface, between 'the two extremes, of too much stiffness in refusing, and of too much easiness in admitting any variation'; but the variation will not be in liturgy but in the whole of her life. That pervading sense of history which is part of the essential Anglican spirit must not be lost, or with it may go both the sense of the continuity of the Church and the sense of proportion which perspective brings. But there must not be 'too much stiffness in refusing' to meet those changes which an unprecedentedly revolutionary age demands.

2

THE ENGLISH FREE CHURCHES

'"Chapel-folk be more hand-in-glove with them above than we,"
said Joseph thoughtfully.'

Thomas Hardy, Far from the Madding Crowd.

The Reformation and English Dissent

THE phrase 'the English Free Churches' can prove misleading. It can suggest a homogeneous character in these
Churches which is only partially true. Certainly they are one
in a number of important ways. They are all 'free' in the
sense of being without state connection. They are all 'Nonconformist', to use the older term, because at one time or
another they have parted company with their fellow Christians who conform to the Church of England by law established. These, however, are only negations. They are one not
only in what they deny, but in much which they affirm. They
all lay great stress on the Evangelical experience of religion,
and to that end emphasise greatly the proclamation of the
saving Word in preaching. They all share, with some small
variations, a tradition of greater spontaneity in public worship than exists in the Church of England. It would, perhaps,
be no exaggeration to say that they are all one also in giving
a primacy to faith rather than to order in the life of the
Church. Thus, while Anglicans would be anxious to know
whether a Church which sought intercommunion with them
were possessed of the historic episcopate, Free Churchmen
would be more concerned with that Church's Evangelical
doctrine than with her order.

These are great possessions in common, and they find

their expression in the almost complete intercommunion which exists between the English Free Churches. And to these things must be added a great deal of shared experience. Their struggle for civil rights, and the need to make common cause on many issues, have done much to weld the Free Churches together.

Nevertheless, the differences between them are very considerable. The Baptist, Congregational and Presbyterian Churches[1] owe their origin directly to the Reformation and represent the heritage of historic Dissent. The Methodist Church is, of course, of far more recent origin, representing a separation from the Church of England towards the close of the eighteenth century. There is also great disparity in size. The Methodist Church has a membership roughly equal to the total of the other three major Free Churches. There is a great dividing line between these Churches in the practice of the sacrament of baptism. The Baptists only administer this sacrament to believers, while the other Free Churches are at one with the Church of England in baptising infants. Church government also represents a major point of difference. The Methodist and Presbyterian Churches are connexional in government, using a hierarchy of church courts for the purpose. The Baptist and Congregational Churches are composed of congregations each finally possessed of independent authority. This enumeration of points of difference of some substance could be considerably extended. Some will emerge, and others already mentioned will be more fully described, in the pages which follow. We turn now to some brief description of the origin of the major English Free Churches, to which must be added some account of two smaller bodies, the Society of Friends and the

[1] As later pages will show, the present Presbyterian Church of England only very partially represents the considerable Presbyterian element in historic Dissent. Of that element much became Arian (Unitarian), in the eighteenth century.

Unitarians which, however different they may be, owe their origin to the same stream of history.

A summary of the Reformation may be given in terms of its two greatest leaders, Luther and Calvin. 'If the first stage of the Reformation was the Lutheran rediscovery of the Gospel, the second stage was the rediscovery of churchmanship which was accomplished in the Genevan theocracy.'[1] (It was in Geneva that John Calvin's conception of the Church was worked out in what may be called a laboratory experiment.) Here were the two immense driving forces of the Reformation, great pistons which caused the wheels of change to turn. Behind these two pistons lay one source of power—the Scriptures. To change the metaphor, Martin Luther, who went back to the great charters of Evangelical Christianity in Paul's letters to the Galatians and the Romans, cut through the fantastic complexities of mediaeval Catholicism with a sword on which was inscribed *sola fide*.[2] By faith alone, and by nothing else, shall a man be justified before his Maker. This was the great liberating word of the Reformation. It is important, especially for those who suspect the word Protestant and all but lament the Reformation, to stress that this was not a diversion from the stream of historic Christianity. It was a cutting back to the bed of the main stream which ran from Christ himself through Paul and Augustine.

Bernard Manning has written of Luther:

> His was an odd kind of greatness, an unusual kind, but a real kind. His greatness lay in his personal religion ... He had that sort of intuitive knowledge of the situation of a devout soul which amounted to religious genius. And so it came about that the thing which mattered most about Luther was not his theology or his churchmanship, but his personal experience of religion.

[1] Horton Davies, *The English Free Churches* (OUP), pp. 13-14.
[2] 'By faith alone', as opposed to 'justification' by good deeds or 'works'.

That is what gave him the position he holds and deserves in modern history.[1]

But 'all Christian experience is ecclesiastical experience'. In what form of Church was this personal experience of justification by faith in Christ alone to be expressed? Luther had no ecclesiastical genius commensurate with his greatness in piety. (It is, as we shall see, one of the most striking facts about the Methodist revival that John Wesley was possessed in almost equal measure of both kinds of genius.) Luther was a prophet who heard God's word; he was no priest in the sense that he could not devise that which would conserve the word.

It was the labours of a younger contemporary of Luther that resulted in a truly ecclesiastical reformation. The work of John Calvin is founded on one tremendous religious insight—the sovereignty of God. His name is most popularly associated with the doctrine of predestination, a doctrine peculiarly abhorrent to the modern mind unless it is found more palatably as 'What the stars foretell' in the corner of a popular magazine. But in the first edition of his great and formative work, *The Institutes of Religion,* there is but the most passing reference to such a doctrine. What Calvin was affirming was the sovereignty of God. But Calvin was a French lawyer; and predestination to damnation, the eventual outcome of this affirmation, may be said to be due to the logical precision of his mind. (We are reminded of a saying of Dr Carnegie Simpson, 'Theology would have done better had it not done so much.')

On the basis of this revelation of the holy will of the sovereign God, John Calvin re-formed the Church. To quote Bernard Manning again:

Calvin perceived that the greatest need of the sixteenth century was a positive ecclesiastical policy... Only a Church with a

[1] *The Making of Modern English Religion* (SCM Press), p. 71.

claim and sphere as wide, an authority as august, a foundation
as venerable and secure, a machinery as efficient, a policy as
subtle, a temper as high, a mission as complete, could replace the
corrupted Church of Rome and hold its own against the secular
State rising everywhere on the ruins of medieval religion.[1]

Protestantism ... is not the opposite of mediaeval catholicism;
it is simply an improved kind of catholicism.[2]

John Calvin was a High Churchman, who found 'an
authority as august, a foundation as venerable and secure',
and, above all, 'a claim as wide' as anything Rome had displayed. He found it in Holy Scripture. If the rediscovery of
Greek literature had opened the way to humanism and the
Renaissance man, it had also opened the pages of the Greek
New Testament afresh and therefore had revealed the simple
origins of the Christian society. It seemed a long road from
Paul and Barnabas and their apostolic labours and sufferings
to the worldly splendours of the Papal Curia; and no shorter
one between the Upper Room or the Breaking of Bread in an
early house church to the magnificent and complex ceremonial of High Mass at St Peter's in Rome.

John Calvin resolved that the sovereign God must be
sovereign in his Church. Only those things which were his
revealed will in Scripture should be found in either the
Church's government or worship. (We may mark here a
contrast with the Lutheran reformation. Luther was content
to admit in worship all that was not explicitly forbidden in
Scripture; Calvin would have nothing admitted which did not
find its express warrant in Scripture. In liturgy the Church
of England is heir to the Lutheran rather than to the Calvinist Reformation.) It must be stressed that John Calvin
did not believe that he 'invented' or devised a new Church.
His task, under God, was to 're-form' the Church after the
scriptural and apostolic pattern. This meant that there must

[1] *Op cit.*, p. 95.
[2] *Essays in Orthodox Dissent* (Independent Press), p. 52.

be two essential marks of the reformed Church. They are liberty from the State and scriptural simplicity. Thus the Church must not be the creature of the State (as Luther was content that it should be). Such a state of things was a denial of 'the Crown Rights of the Redeemer'. Again, the liturgy and order of a truly reformed Church must be such as revealed rather than obscured the central saving acts of God in Jesus Christ.

In this country Calvinism took two forms, *Presbyterian* and *Congregationalist*. The first possessed the normal, centralised kind of church order. Chiefly this was found within the Church of England itself, battling over a long period from within to make the English Reformation take the Presbyterian turning. Thus there was a long period during which 'classes' or embryonic presbyteries were to be found in parts of the country within the national Church. It was, however, a peculiar feature of the English religious scene to see developed a decentralised form of Calvinism in the form of the Independents, or Brownists.[1] They are the direct ancestors of our present-day Congregationalists. They were Calvinist in doctrine, but believed that Christ reigned in his Church not through the graduated series of church courts found in Presbyterianism but through his guiding presence in each individual covenanted fellowship of believers. Hence their successive names of Independent and Congregationalist.

The third strand in historic Dissent is provided by *the Baptists*. The Anabaptists, or 're-baptisers', appeared on the left wing of the continental Reformation, objecting that there was no warrant in Scripture for the baptism of infants. From 1525 onwards they began to form separate groups. Before long their ideas spread to England. But it was on the Continent, in Holland, that the first English Baptist congregation was established, by Thomas Helwys in 1612. It was his-

---

[1] So-called from Robert Browne (c. 1550-1633), the first man to expound this form of churchmanship.

torically the result of a separation from an Independent or Separatist[1] congregation, and the Baptist churches continued to share this form of church government with the Congregationalists. It would be wrong nevertheless to think of the Baptists as merely Congregationalists with a different conviction about the sacrament of baptism. They represented an even more radical side of the Reformation, with more drastic views on liturgy and more emphasis upon apocalyptic hopes. Any kind of set worship was to them almost satanic. Until the early eighteenth century English Baptist congregations were only with difficulty persuaded even to sing in unison, since this implied a denial of spontaneity!

The Churchmanship of Dissent

It is plainly impossible to describe here the history of English Dissent. But one essential point must now be made arising from this brief account of their origins, before the outline of the continuing story is sketched.

This is that *all three types of English Dissent were 'High Church'*. This may seem odd both to those who stand within their traditions today to whom that phrase is almost a synonym for 'the hidden hand of Rome', and those who, on the other hand, deny to those traditions the name of 'church' at all. It is because of this common misunderstanding that the point is so essential. Neither Presbyterian, Independent nor Baptist could tolerate a doctrine of the Church that saw it as comprising all those who were citizens of a nominally Christian nation, making Christ's Church merely the nation under a spiritual aspect. Perhaps the Presbyterian appeared to come nearer to doing this than the others, but this was only because he saw the ideal state as a theocracy, a 'rule of the saints', in which in fact the Church controlled the State rather than the State the Church. The Independents and Baptists were emphatic that the Church could only

[1] This was the description then used.

consist of Christians, those, that is, whom Christ had gathered out of the world. They were 'gathered' churches. They and the Presbyterians shared the conviction that the Church of Jesus Christ could acknowledge only one Head—Christ himself. This is put succinctly in the words of a question addressed by the Presbytery to the present author at his ordination to the ministry of word and sacraments:

> Are you persuaded that the Lord Jesus Christ, the only King and Head of the Church, has therein appointed a government distinct from civil government, and in things spiritual not subordinate thereto; and that rulers, while bound to render obedience to Christ in their own province, ought not to constrain men's religious belief or invade the rights of conscience?

They were High Church, too, in another sense. Principal John Marsh sums it up thus:

> They are 'High Church' because they believe that it is to the whole Church, not to some one person or some one class or order within the Church that Christ authoritatively reveals his will; and they must be reckoned High Churchmen because they all believe that it is the duty of every member to share both in the seeking for the guidance of the will of Christ and in the hearing and acceptance of any testimony by any member or officer as to the specification of the will of Christ in any circumstances at any time.[1]

In English Dissent the layman came into his own. Calvin did not destroy the distinction between the ministry and the laity:[2] indeed he taught a very high conception of the ministerial office and prescribed a very thorough training for it. What he did destroy was the whole idea of different grades of Christian obedience, one for those in orders and another

---

[1] *Essays in Anglican Self-Criticism*, p. 185.

[2] I am, of course, aware of the current ecumenical emphasis upon the laity, the 'laos', being the *whole* people of God, i.e., ministry and what are customarily called 'laity'. As the minister of a Calvinist Church, I am wholly happy with it, but we lack any word to describe the 'laos' without the parsons. Meanwhile 'laity' must serve in its normally accepted sense.

for the rest. To the Calvinist mind the phrase 'the religious life' used as a description for monasticism is utterly offensive. Every man in his particular calling seeking to serve God is 'a religious'. The doctrine of the 'calling' is central in Calvinism, and finds its most concrete expression in the office of the elder. The elder is a man who is ordained to spiritual office for life while continuing to earn his daily bread through his calling. He continues in the popular sense to live the life of a layman. At every point, however, in a Presbyterian church he is joined with the minister of word and sacraments, in the offices both of rule and of pastoral care. Presbyterianism, as has been said, consists of a hierarchy of church courts. Locally the congregation is ruled and guided by the session, a court consisting of the elders presided over by the minister. The elders locally have in addition to this function of rule, a pastoral and, in modern times, a liturgical office. Each elder will have a district of the congregation which he visits in the name of the Church. At the observance of the sacrament of the Lord's Supper he bears out the elements of bread and wine to the people. Regionally the Church is governed by the presbytery, and on this an equal number of elders sit with the ministers. Nationally the same is true for the General Assembly. There are no matters which come before church courts—such as decisions on doctrine— reserved for the ministers.[1]

In Churches of independent polity—Congregational or Baptist—the place of the laity is even more prominent. The church meeting, through which the members seek to discharge the high conception of their privileges set out by Dr Marsh, is not intended to be democratic, but Christocratic. Thus there has always been a great reluctance to proceed in

---

[1] The office of moderator (as the presiding officer of a church court is known) seems by inviolable custom reserved for the ministry, and the method of conduct of worship is wholly the prerogative of the minister of the congregation.

serious matters by the normal democratic procedures of resolution and amendment and decision by majority vote. Rather has the company been called to wait upon God to guide them to a common mind. The question concerning this doctrine of membership in the Body of Christ is not whether it is high enough, but whether it is not too high for mortal men. It was a Congregational scholar, Dr W. B. Selbie, who made the following comment upon the original exiled Church in Holland:

> But the story of the Church in Holland is not altogether an edifying one. The Independent or Congregational system is one that requires a truly Christian standard of conduct if it is to be successfully maintained. Where this is absent it invariably breaks down.[1]

Although the Independent system was not primarily intended to be democratic, any more than the Presbyterian was intended to be an ecclesiastical parliamentary system, it is obvious that both set such value upon the voice of the laity as to be unpalatable either to Tudor or to Stuart pretensions. But such was the spirit of the age that when in the period of the Commonwealth power fell into their hands they proved to have no more tolerance than those who had discriminated against them. The fact remains that the opportunity for magnanimity which came at the time of the Restoration was tragically lost. The penal acts against Nonconformists known as the Clarendon Code, and the Great Ejectment in 1662 in which well over two thousand ministers, chiefly Presbyterians and Independents, were thrust out from their livings, at one stroke destroyed the possibility of any national unity in religion, and made Nonconformity a political force. Henceforth the struggle to possess civil liberties could have no other issue.

The continuing story of the fortunes of Dissent until the coming into being of by far the greatest of the English Free

[1] *Nonconformity* (Williams and Norgate), p. 52.

Churches, the Methodist, is a mixed one. It gave to English piety one of the two greatest of her hymn writers, Isaac Watts, and in John Bunyan (for whose ecclesiastical allegiance Congregational and Baptist scholars still strive) incomparably the greatest allegorist to use the English tongue. His influence on the Christian thinking of the English people is probably only exceeded by Scripture itself and the Book of Common Prayer. It was his supreme gift to make vivid and personal the whole teaching of orthodox Puritan piety. Speaking of Christian with his burden, G. M. Trevelyan writes:

> That lonely figure, with the Bible and the burden of sin, is not only John Bunyan himself. It is the representative Puritan of the English Puritan epoch . . . That man, multiplied, congregated, regimented, was a force of tremendous potency, to make and to destroy. It was the force by which Oliver Cromwell and George Fox and John Wesley wrought their wonders, being men of a like experience themselves.[1]

A man like Bunyan who makes articulate that experience in unforgettable picture and adventure has done more than describe it. He has enlarged and released its power.

If Bunyan supplied the story, Watts supplied the song, a song which in Bernard Manning's words sounds 'the august notes of true Catholic theology and true Christian living'.[2] In the spiritual doldrums of the eighteenth century it was much to have a writer who could set on men's lips

> When I survey the wondrous Cross,
> On which the Prince of glory died

or

> This holy bread and wine
>   Maintains our fainting breath
> By union with our living Lord
>   And interest in His death.

---

[1] *English Social History* (Longmans), pp. 234-5.
[2] *The Hymns of Wesley and Watts* (Epworth Press), p. 103.

Unitarians and Friends

It has rightly been claimed that it was these two writers, Bunyan and Watts, who did most to keep Independency orthodox when Presbyterianism was lapsing into Arianism.[1] Doubtless in a day of penal codes which forbade the assembling of the wider courts of the Church Presbyterianism was in greater danger than a system which by belief centred authority in the local congregation. Be that as it may, it is from the eighteenth century, and largely from English Presbyterian congregations, that Unitarianism arose. The main stress of Unitarian Churches, it is only fair to say, has not been hostility to Trinitarian views, but opposition to any kind of credal definition or tests which would limit the spirit of enquiry. The Churches which owe their origin to diverse movements formed a denomination in 1928 when a General Assembly of Unitarian and Free Christian Churches was instituted. Today it numbers in its fellowship only about twenty-eight thousand, but Unitarian families like the Holts and Rathbones of Liverpool, and the Chamberlains of Birmingham, have played a considerable part in modern English history. Thinkers like James Martineau and, more recently, L. P. Jacks, have exercised an influence far beyond the bounds of their denomination—whose formal existence, incidentally, L. P. Jacks deplored, regarding the forming of the General Assembly as contrary to the spirit of freedom in the churches of that tradition.

The other and earlier departure from English Dissent shared the Unitarian dislike of confessions, creeds and formularies, but in almost every way was at the other extreme from the temper of the Arian developments. This was the Society of Friends, or as they are popularly known, by a nickname they early came to accept, the Quakers.

[1] The denial of Christ's full divinity associated with the heretic Arius.

The originator of this body was George Fox (1621-1691). He might be called a Nonconformist to Nonconformity. Just as the earlier Dissenters had revolted against the formality of the Church of England, so Fox now revolted against both as being without the Spirit. It is not easy to reconcile the gravity and sobriety of the typical Quaker of history, or indeed the characteristic contemporary Quaker, with the wild and radical figure of the founder of the body. His out-right condemnation of the normal churches which he called 'steeple-houses', his altercations in church with preachers who did not to his mind preach the Gospel aright, and his barefoot journey through Lichfield uttering the chilling shout, 'Woe unto the bloody city of Lichfield!' seem a far cry from the decorous behaviour of Frys, Cadburys and Rowntrees, those Quakers who, as Dr Horton Davies charmingly remarks, 'may be said to have sweetened both diet and business relationships'. But this was only a contrast of appearances. Fox fought battles which his later followers did not need to fight. His teaching had from the beginning the germs of all the characteristic Quaker positions. He had immense social concern, being interested in prison conditions (as well he might be, having been imprisoned for a total of eight years in some six different jails) and the care of the poor and the aged. He utterly rejected all the pretensions of human rank, and taught his followers to address one another in the second person singular, and to dress without ostentation. He declared the impossibility of participation in war for a Christian. Above all, he recovered the doctrine of the Holy Spirit as Christian experience with his teaching of the Inner Light. Quaker worship was, and is, dependent upon nothing but the Spirit's inspiration given to individual worshippers. All else is silence. It is the standing refutation of what has been called the current image of the Christian Church—a parson talking. Although the Society never, except in the closing years of George Fox's life, became a large body, or indeed, save for a brief and uncharacteristic period, a body seeking its own enlargement, it has played a part in English religious development utterly disproportionate to the number within its fellowship.

John Wesley and Methodism

We now come to the formation of the Methodist Church. In the previous chapter we have recognised that this movement was intended by God to be one of Evangelical revival and spiritual renewal within the Church of England. Although linked with a distinguished Dissenting family through his mother, the redoubtable Susannah, John Wesley's whole background was characteristically Anglican, and High Church Anglican at that. It was the Anglicanism of the Caroline divines, and of the Non-Jurors, those bishops who had for conscience' sake refused to acknowledge Dutch William as true King of England. Born in 1703, he came from a Lincolnshire country rectory, and was educated at Oxford. The pathetic failure of his period of service in Georgia was identical in pattern with that which might attend the prickly efforts of an arrogantly 'spiky' curate today. What he also possessed was a profound seriousness in religion, which showed itself in the rigid discipline to which he and his associates submitted themselves in the Holy Club they formed at Oxford, and in his sensitiveness to the challenge of the quality of life of the Moravian missionaries on shipboard when he was returning from the collapse of his ministry in the New World. The Moravians, a small body of Lutheran origin with intense missionary convictions, have never been numerous in Britain and have only become established in certain districts. They can, however, claim a large place in Christian history as God's midwives who brought the Methodist revival to birth.[1] It was at a Moravian meeting

[1] They can also claim in James Montgomery a hymn-writer who, if we exclude Charles Wesley and Watts, can stand comparison with any.

in Aldersgate Street in the City of London in 1738, while study was being made of Luther's commentary on the epistle to the Romans, that John Wesley's heart was 'strangely warmed', probably the most influential religious experience since Luther himself had found the peace he sought in justification by faith in Christ alone. So did the disciplined and ordered training of Wesley's Anglican heritage provide a fertile and prepared ground into which the seed of an intense recovery of Luther's great conviction could be received and fructify. Martin Luther's chief contribution to English religion came not at the Reformation, but centuries later through the Methodist revival.

So there began the fascinating saga of John Wesley's ceaseless journeyings throughout the British Isles. Non-Methodists are apt to smile at the continuous flow of Wesleyana that pours from the printing presses to meet what seems to be an unquenchable thirst for knowledge about the founder of the Methodist society. But a small acquaintance with its subject affords a worthier explanation of this than denominational hagiography. He is not only incomparably the most influential English figure in the religious story of the world, but a man of infinite fascination. A preacher of amazing power, an organiser of genius and an author of singular range, he was possessed of a tireless energy that enabled him throughout a long life to do the work of several men. When to him was joined a younger brother, Charles, to act as laureate of the revival, an irresistible force was created. Charles was a person of far less personal quality, but his genius as a hymnwriter is only equalled by Isaac Watts himself. 'Methodism was born in song,' the preface of the present *Methodist Hymnbook* roundly begins. It was true. Charles Wesley had written at his conversion a hymn which John and others joined in singing on the very night when John received his assurance of God's forgiveness in the meeting at Aldersgate Street:

> Where shall my wondering soul begin?
> How shall I all to heaven aspire?
> A slave redeemed from death and sin,
> A brand plucked from eternal fire,
> How shall I equal triumphs raise,
> Or sing my great Deliverer's praise?

Here are the authentic notes of the Methodist revival. Wonder is one of them. (Professor Gordon Rupp has well said that '. . . at its best not awe but wonder is the keynote of Nonconformist worship'.[1] This is certainly true of Methodism.) Redemption and sheer deliverance is another. The utterly personal note is the third. The first person singular is used in much of characteristic Methodist hymnody.

These three notes challenged the common religious assumptions of the day. Wonder was little encouraged by a Deism that had reduced Almighty God to a presumed First Cause. Redemption and deliverance, especially expressed by such coarse metaphors as slavery and eternal fire, were repellent to the rationalistic temper of the time. And that religion should be a living personal encounter of the soul with its Maker was a thought almost forgotten.

Of course the Wesleys were not alone in experiencing a great Evangelical awakening. There were others, some of whom joined with them, and others of whom worked alone, sometimes repelled by what they judged to be excesses, permitted if not encouraged by the Wesleys. John Wesley nevertheless stands supreme by his achievement in making the Christian faith a vibrant power in the land. Although we may consider him not immune from the preacher's common disability when counting his congregation of being able to multiply without being able to subtract, it is clear that no man before the age of mass communication can have been heard declaring the Gospel by so many. He came just when the new industrial populations were beginning to grow up

[1] *Six Makers of English Religion* (Hodder & Stoughton), p. 118.

around the coal fields and the manufacturing centres; when England had begun that remorseless march from a rural to an urban economy which was to exact so grim a toll in human life and happiness. And this fastidious Oxford don, after an inward struggle, 'submitted to be more vile' and began to preach not only in those parish churches that would receive him but in the open air to the miners and the rest.

He callenged the current Calvinism as well as the easy-going Deism, and for his pains was called by the author of *Rock of Ages* 'that low and puny tadpole in divinity'. He declared that God's free salvation in Christ was offered to all men. All that a man must do was believe, and trust that Christ could forgive his sins. He was not a preacher who belittled the sacraments in exalting the Word. He believed that the Holy Communion was 'a converting ordinance', and sought its celebration with far greater frequency than was common in contemporary Anglicanism.

His emphasis on sanctification was no less than that on justification. He sought to build men up in scriptural holiness. Although, especially in Cornwall, there may have been out-breaks of antinomianism,[1] this was an utter perversion of true Methodism, which has had a strong and continuing emphasis upon personal and social ethics.

It is possible, however, that much of the irrigating stream of new life which Wesley brought to English religion might have been lost had he not possessed, as he did, a remarkable power to canalise it. 'In John Wesley,' says Bernard Manning, 'the Methodists had a leader who, by a stroke of divine genius that puts him in the same rank as Hildebrand, St Dominic and St Ignatius Loyola, combined the evangelical passion and experience of Luther with Calvin's ecclesiastical system.'[2] This was his large framework, as it were. He built up a Pres-

---

[1] The idea that since God's grace is all that matters the moral law can be disregarded.
[2] *The Making of Modern English Religion*, pp. 109-110.

byterian system of church government for his society, although it was founded not upon a Calvinist but a Lutheran or Arminian[1] theology.

Nevertheless his genius appears as much in apparently smaller matters. He did not just beseech converted men to grow in scriptural holiness. He gathered them into little classes, making payment for the class ticket the way of contributing to the maintenance of the society, and the class-meeting itself an occasion for testimony and mutual support in the Christian life. He did not just ask men to believe sound doctrine. He, with the chief instrumentality of his brother, set it upon their lips in song. In 1780 he published *A Collection of Hymns for the Use of the People called Methodists*. Of this publication Bernard Manning has written:

> This little book ... ranks in Christian literature with the Psalms, the Book of Common Prayer, the Canon of the Mass. In its own way, it is perfect, unapproachable, elemental in its perfection. You cannot alter it except to mar it; it is a work of supreme devotional art by a religious genius.[2]

These seem the words of hyperbole. To read the index of the 1780 hymnal is to recognise their substantial truth. Our particular point here, however, is that Wesley was right to claim that in this little book he had given his followers 'a little body of experimental and practical divinity'. It was an essential instrument in establishing Christian men in sound doctrine and holy living.

The obduracy of the Church of England brought about the separate development of the Methodist society as a Church.

[1] Arminius (1560-1609) reacted against the harsher side of Calvinism, notably the doctrine of predestination.
[2] *The Hymns of Wesley and Watts*, p. 14.
I cannot bring myself to apologise for what may seem excessive quotation from Manning's books, so small in volume and so rich in content. If it leads any readers to make personal acquaintance with them they will be led to a deeper understanding of what the English Free Churches have been in our national religious life than anything else will afford.

It is to Wesley's credit that the steps which led to the break, culminating in his ordination of preachers for North America, were taken with the greatest reluctance. It was possibly too much to hope that the bishops of the Church of the day, largely dwelling in prelatical splendour, should have sought ways to accommodate religious practices as repellent in their vulgarity as lay preaching, extempore prayer, preaching in the fields and the hysterical ejaculations of those under conviction of sin. The effect of their failure was to make the division between those who conformed to the national Church and those who did not a much more equal one than it would have been without the split, perhaps the gravest tragedy in the story of British religion.

The subsequent history of Methodism is one of successive division and then, in this century, of reunion. The Methodist New Connexion was formed in 1797, six years after the founder's death, largely as a lay protest against excessive clericalism. (John Wesley, for all his use of the lay preacher, had some ingrained Anglican attitudes which remained in the legacy of his organisation.) Other secessions took place early in the nineteenth century, the most notable being that which led to the formation of the Primitive Methodist Connexion in 1820. It is an ironical commentary on the conservative trend of all religious organisations that the ground of their action was refusal to obey the behest of the Wesleyan Conference not to hold open-air revival meetings—a practice which does not seem notably contrary to the mind of the founder. The smaller secessions (with the exception of the small Wesleyan Reform Union and Independent Methodist Church, which retain separate existence to the present time) united to form the United Methodist Church in 1907. This Church, together with the Primitive Methodist Connexion, joined in 1932 with the parent Wesleyan Methodist Church to form Methodism as we know it today. It is worthwhile recalling this history, for splendidly united as the present

Church has become, without some such knowledge such common references as 'Of course, he's ex-Prim' would be mystifying indeed.

Nonconformity's Glory and Decline

The glorious years of Nonconformity were during the later nineteenth century, and the glory spilt over into the first decade of this. It is impossible to understand the situation —we had almost said 'plight'—of the English Free Churches today unless it is seen in contrast with the years of prosperity in whose afterglow the older amongst us grew up, and the physical equipment of which remains to hamper and daunt us.

During the last century the population of Britain quadrupled, and from being a dominantly rural country we became a dominantly urban one. The very untramelled character of the Free Churches gave them flexibility in dealing with so revolutionary a situation. As the Bishop of Middleton puts it:

> The Methodists had complete local freedom to develop in their own flexible way; their buildings could be makeshift and economical; they could start 'causes' or stop them, or remove them elsewhere, and above all they were rooted in local groups far too small to be considered for episcopal chapels of ease. They required only a preacher, who could be a layman, and zeal — and they had both. Where the National Church required an Act of Parliament, a grant of money, an educated gentleman and a crop of lawyers, the Methodists required only a friendly barn and a zealous preacher![1]

The older Dissent tended to be more *bourgeois*. But both in fact were linked with rising forces in the social revolution which marked the later decades of the century. Although the original Wesleyan Methodism remained conservative and even reactionary in politics, the smaller Methodist groups

---

[1] E. R. Wickham, *Church and People in an Industrial City* (Lutterworth), p. 80.

were more socially radical and had direct links (as had other branches of Nonconformity) with Chartism and other efforts to secure justice for the workers in mine and factory. Again, the immense expansion of industry and commerce meant an enormous increase in the middle classes and in that *petit bourgeoisie* which supplied the necessary army of clerks and the like. The more powerful middle classes resented the dominion of privilege and therefore allied themselves with the struggle of the Nonconformist Churches to be rid of the remaining civil disabilities which they endured. The *petit bourgeoisie* found in the chapel not only a place of religious fellowship but, increasingly as the century wore on, a centre of real and popular culture. And all found in the chapels a sphere where gifts could be exercised and developed. Earlier in this chapter we have emphasised that Independency, for example, was intended to express Christocracy, not to foster democracy. Nevertheless, experience in democratic ways was an obvious by-product of the church meeting, and tenure of such offices as that of deacon gave experience in the handling of affairs. Methodism, with its far more extensive use of the layman as preacher, trained a great number of men to be articulate in the service of the Church. Their capacity for expressing themselves was applicable to other ranges of activity. In a multitude of ways the Nonconformist Churches were educative.

Readers of Nonconformist religious literature of the turn of the century also derive an unmistakable impression that Nonconformity felt history to be on its side. Sacerdotal and state religion could not but wither and die under the impact of new knowledge and a democratic society. The future must lie with a religion unhampered and prophetic. Disestablishment was but a matter of time, and a short time at that. One by one the remaining bastions of Erastian[1] privilege—church rates, discriminatory burial laws and so forth—had been

[1] The ascendancy of the State over the Church.

removed. The time must be near when the whole structure of privilege would be no more. Nonconformity was conscious of power.

That power was no delusion right until the First World War. It is less than half a century since the editor of a Free Church paper, *The British Weekly,* was a constant and influential visitor at the Prime Minister's breakfast table. Earlier it was popularly said that Birmingham was governed from Dr Dale's vestry in Carr's Lane Chapel. The power of Nonconformity was particularly great in the new manufacturing towns which had grown up away from long-established church centres. The Nonconformist vote was zealously wooed by political parties. And all this has gone within the lifetime of the older amongst us, and left but a bewildered nostalgia behind.

> It is probable that Nonconformity reached its height of political power, was most representative of the temper of the English people, round the beginning of this century ... But in the generation that has passed since the great liberal landslide of 1906, one of the greatest changes in the English religious and social landscape has been the decline of Nonconformity.[1]

Professor Brogan's judgment is sober truth. The reasons for the steep decline are not easy to assess. One considerable one undoubtedly was the far too close identification of more militant Nonconformity with political liberalism. There were readily understandable historical reasons for this. 'Persecution under the Stuarts was succeeded by toleration under William III. Consequently the Dissenters associated tyranny with the Tories, and liberty with the Whigs. For this reason Nonconformity threw in its lot with the Whigs of the eighteenth century and the Liberals of the nineteenth.'[2] This was all very well when the cause of liberal reform was a struggling

[1] D. W. Brogan, *The English People* (Hamish Hamilton), p. 121.
[2] Horton Davies, *The English Free Churches,* pp. 102-3.

one. It was even all right when it was winning its victories. It was fatal once they had been won. As Dr E. A. Payne points out,

> At the very time. . . that the workers became increasingly class-conscious and determined on the redress of their wrongs, the Nonconformist bodies achieved victory in their own struggle for religious equality and became respectable and prosperous. It is difficult not to trace a connection between, on the one hand, the new social opportunities which came to Free Churchmen and the increasing funds at their disposal, and, on the other, a gradual alienation from the working classes, though there were clearly many other causes at work as well.[1]

It is notoriously difficult to judge the relationship of Churches to social classes. The accusation is often levelled at Methodism that it ceased to be a proletarian Church and became a bourgeois one. Even if that be true, it leaves unanswered the question whether Methodism abandoned the working class or transformed it, by the inculcation of thrift, industry, sobriety and family feeling, into something else. We suspect the latter process to be the truth, although it leaves unanswered the question why it did not continue. But even rejecting all glib judgments there is a point of failure in Nonconformity at the time of liberal decline. It became respectable, settled and in a situation of profound spiritual danger. It had pulled down its barns and built greater ones, and the night of the Great War demanded its soul.

The decline in membership of the Free Churches has been great. It is normally recognised that the Baptist Churches have particularly reliable statistics, since membership of them is based upon so definite a personal confession of faith. In 1906 the membership is given as 434,741. In 1957 it was but 327,048. Even more steep was the decline in the number

[1] *The Free Church Tradition in the Life of England* (SCM Press), p. 128.

of Sunday school scholars. In 1906 it was 590,321. In 1957 it was little more than half that figure, 310,696—and the rate of decline was accelerating. At the time of Methodist union in 1932 there were 838,019 members of societies. In 1959 there were only 733,658. The Congregational Churches, which were most closely allied with political Nonconformity, have perhaps naturally suffered worst of all. In 1909 they had 456,613 members. Fifty years later that number had sunk to 212,017. During the half-century 1901-1951 the population of England and Wales grew from 32,527,843 to 43,758,000.

Of course the period in question has been one of steep decline in religious observance in the whole community; but the evidence seems inescapable that the Free Churches have suffered it more severely in fact, and also felt in more acutely because of the preceding period of great expansion and large expectations.

One strong, if not obvious, contributory factor has been the lessening of the place of oratory in public life. Even before Stanley Baldwin, with perhaps more even than his customary dissembling, called it 'the harlot of the arts', the change had come. The intimacy of address to which people became accustomed through broadcasting was a potent factor in bringing about this change. Much more influential was the suspicion which attended the large persuasions which the orator sought to effect. The horrors of the First World War had engendered a pervasive scepticism which resisted the art of rhetoric. This had a profound effect upon the Free Churches, whose leaders had been the great pulpit orators. Nothing could be more ludicrous than to suggest that they were merely loquacious hypocrites. Some of them were spiritual giants— men like Dale of Birmingham who was preacher, scholar and statesman combined. They made large demands upon the intelligence of their hearers, and these demands were gladly met. There was, as we have suggested, a strong will to be educated and enlightened as well as uplifted among much of nineteenth-century Nonconformity. But there was also something of entertainment at its best in the days of the pulpit giants. Charles Haddon Spurgeon may be accounted possibly the greatest natural genius of the pulpit that England has produced. His influence for good in South London and beyond is as incalculable as his range of homiletic power was immense; but he was also a great entertainer, using every artifice of wit, humour, ingenuity and dramatic daring to drive home his message. Thus he, and others who shared in any measure his gifts, had an immediate attraction for the generality of men before the days of mass entertainment.

All this has gone. There are other, and more meretricious, sources of popular entertainment; and, at a more serious level, men seem to turn more readily for religious enlightenment to the paperback than to the pulpit. In England the day of pulpit oratory seems done, and it is perhaps significant that the most famous of contemporary Free Church preachers, Dr Leslie Weatherhead, has always spoken more in the intimate manner of a man broadcasting.

It would be difficult to over-emphasise the effect of this on the Free Churches. During the nineteenth century their leadership was a leadership through the pulpit. While the Church of England might catch the ear of the general public through the claim of a man's office—as Archbishop of Canterbury or Bishop of London—the Free Churches did it through their outstanding preachers. The utterances of Hugh Price Hughes, Charles Haddon Spurgeon, R. W. Dale, F. B. Meyer or later, J. H. Jowett, were news. Of possibly only one Free Churchman can that be said to-day—Dr Donald Soper of the Methodist West London Mission—and this chiefly because of his social and political radicalism.

Another and allied factor has been the evacuation by the Free Churches of the centre of many cities. There is much to be said for the view that a man should worship where he lives, and not forsake his community to trek to the city centre to be beguiled by a fashionable preacher. But it is naturally difficult to exercise any national influence from a suburb. A hierarchical Church like the Church of England, possessing its officers with representative and historic titles and cathedrals which act as the natural focus for large occasions of religious observance, does not suffer the same disadvantage as its worshippers move out to ever more distant suburbs.

Nevertheless the chief reasons for the steeper rate of Free Church decline must be found elsewhere. If the First World War made most men suspicious of the claims of all authority, it also paradoxically made those who were drawn to the Christian religion prefer a form of it which claimed a definite authority. The Free Churches, which had tended to set the authority of Holy Scripture where Rome had set the Church, had been compelled to face the challenge of the results of biblical criticism. It is indeed one of their glories that, having for so long been excluded from the ancient universities, their contribution to the new study of the Scriptures and to the reconciliation of the emerging position with Evangelical religion was so great. It would, however, be foolish to deny that for many Free Churches in the earlier part of this century there was something of an abandonment of their historic Evangelical and High Church position. Individualism was the fruit of a liberalism in decay. There was much talk of fellowship and the Kingdom, but little of the Church. Among Congregationalists there were those who did not desire to be baptised or to partake of the Lord's Supper. And curiously with the individualistic emphasis could go a proclamation of a 'social gospel' which was certainly needed, but which was insufficiently rooted in the great Christian verities of man's fallen nature and need for divine salvation.

With these uncertainties went also a collapse of some of the old disciplines. Historic Nonconformity had rejected the observance of the Christian Year, which had indeed become

cluttered with observances 'unknown to Holy Scripture or
to venerable tradition'. That meant that there was, for
example, no fasting for Lent. There was however a far more
regular and demanding discipline in the observance of the
Lord's Day, given almost wholly to worship and edifying
activity. Along with other Churches Nonconformity has
experienced a considerable lessening of such Puritan rigour,
which few will regret. Its effect nonetheless has been to leave
the Free Churches needing a new form of discipline. It was
an Anglican bishop, but no unfriendly critic, being the son of
a most distinguished Congregational father who has always
prized his paternal inheritance, who remarked:

> The sad decline in the vigour of Free Church worship seems to
> have dated from the passing of the Puritan Sabbath, for it left
> Free Churchmen with no other discipline of worship. It all be-
> came too easy among the middle classes. Morning church after
> a late breakfast; none of the discomfort of kneeling when you
> got there; apart from hymn-singing, which tended to become
> more and more sentimental, no vigorous call to participate in a
> liturgy of the people. Little demand, and so slackening response.[1]

The Worship of the Free Churches

Our last few paragraphs may be judged by some to be a
premature and impious funeral sermon on the Free Churches,
whose demise has not yet been announced. Nothing could be
further from our purpose, but it would be plainly dishonest
in a book on the British Churches today not to take seriously
the great change which has come over the English religious
scene by the great diminution both of the Free Churches and
of their place in the national life. In fact, it is unlikely that
the Free Churches will know the renewal which would enable
them to bring their great contribution to the Coming Great
Church of the future unless there is a far more drastic analysis

[1] Leslie S. Hunter, Bishop of Sheffield, *The Seed and the Fruit*
(SCM Press), p. 79.

of their present condition. From that should come the willingness to recover that resilience and flexibility which ought to characterise them, in order to serve the present age. There are some signs that this is happening.

There has been for a long time a deeper interest in the ordering of worship. Of course there are those who decry this as an arid concern with forms, when the glory of Free Church worship has been its free spontaneous response to the movement of the Spirit. The age and strength of that tradition of extempore prayer are undeniable. It is a tradition which lends itself to the ready sneers of the top-lofty; but those who are bred on it will find again and again that it opens the gates of heaven for the worshipping company of Christ's people. W. R. Maltby's description of his old minister praying gives a moving picture of what such prayer can be:

> I remember those opening sentences when he pushed off into the deep, until the heavenly breath caught the sail, and bore us away to the things that are unseen and eternal. Oh, those wide and open seas! Those awful depths! That majestic firmament! And that frail barque amid so mighty a sea! And what tempestuous thoughts tossed the soul! And still through all the buffetings of conscience and the conflict of hopes and fears, that man would cry for himself and for us all, pleading the promises and still prevailing, till at last he turned us homeward again ... I remember that we used to look at him when it was over, but he didn't look at us; and now I could guess the reason why.[1]

The comment which this invites is, 'Oh, but not every minister is a devotional genius like that.' This is true, but the members of Churches possessing a set liturgy will not truly appreciate the attachment of the Free Churches (and, incidentally, in large measure the Church of Scotland) to extempore prayer unless they see it rooted in belief in the Holy Spirit. It is not desire for a ministerial monologue which has precluded set forms of prayer, but conviction that God the Holy Spirit could take the rough, half-formed petitions of

[1] *Obiter Scripta* (Epworth Press), p. 105.

frail but sincere men and make them wide channels of his mercy. It would be a sad loss indeed if the Free Churches lost their tradition of free prayer, either by wholly abandoning it for prescribed forms, or allowing it to decline, as it sometimes does, into an ossified and poorly phrased liturgy. The Church of God today needs more and not less emphasis upon the immediacy of that experience of the Holy Spirit which can be known within the fellowship.

It remains doubtful, however, whether such prayer should be the sole diet of Christian congregations. For where this is so the congregation is put very much at the minister's mercy. Extempore prayer can be too subjective and ruminative for the congregation readily to make their own. This has been recognised in this century by the production of many books of prayers and services both officially by the Free Churches and unofficially by ministers of them. Notable among the latter was John Hunter's *Devotional Services* (issued in its best known edition in 1901), which was not only a pioneering book, but combines in rare fashion the qualities of contemporaneity and beauty. *The Book of Common Order* (1940) of the Church of Scotland has had great influence south as well as north of the border. None of these books, it must be emphasised, are obligatory. There can be few congregations where any of their set forms is followed Sunday by Sunday. What they provide is both material and standards for the conduct of public worship. In these regards their influence has been immense. It is an ill-ordered Free Church service today which appears merely to be a 'hymn-sandwich'. The ordered progress of the prayers through invocation, adoration, confession, thanksgiving, petition and intercession should be visible, even if unobtrusive. The choice of hymns should not be as arbitrary as it sometimes is in Anglican worship, but should mark a movement of feeling and purpose. This is all the more important when the people's part in the offering of worship is so often limited to the praise.

For while the production of many books of prayers and services has enriched the devotional material on which the minister has drawn, and helped a right ordering of worship, it has done little to enable the congregation to play any vocal part in prayer. This, to be fully achieved, would require books to be set into the hands of the congregation, and this has been but little done.

It may still be wondered whether sufficient has been done by the use of such simple methods as the bidding, silence and readily learned response. What is really in doubt is whether the Free Churches have remained sufficiently free in their use of ways of prayer, or have become as hidebound as any liturgical Church. Certainly today there has been a diminution of the power of giving attention to utterance of any kind. This has greatly lessened the ability, especially of younger people, to 'make their own' long prayers offered in the minister's words alone. This is recognised in Sunday school departments, where responsive prayer is normal. It is strange that it should continue to be little recognised in the Churches' normal worship.

A considerable change is also coming to the hymnody of the Free Churches. The dominance of the subjective, individualistic and sometimes strained hymn of the Victorian era is diminishing as new hymn-books emerge. *The Methodist Hymnbook* is obviously a compromise book, rightly choosing the way of comprehension when three Methodist bodies has just been united. It contains great treasure from the Wesleys, but is undoubtedly filled out by a good deal that is in comparison dross. *Congregational Praise* (1951) shows well the new stress upon the hymn which is objective, scriptural and truly adapted for corporate worship. Rumour has it that the new book for the use of the Baptists, at present being prepared for publication, will further demonstrate this more healthy trend.

A natural further stage in this whole process of liturgical

recovery is the restoration of the Christian Year. This is a remarkably recent movement, and is making progress by leaps and bounds. It would be difficult today to have the experience of which we heard complaint just before the war, that a certain worshipper had attended a Free Church on Easter Day without hearing any reference to the resurrection of our Lord. Not only are Christmas Day, Good Friday, Easter Day and Whitsuntide commonly fully observed, but the practice of Holy Week services, and the marking of Ascensiontide and All Saints' Day, are growing. In these and in other ways the Free Churches experience the influence of the Liturgical Movement which is coming to affect every Church.

Congregationalism Today

It has been reasonable in the consideration of the present position of the Free Churches in England to speak of them together. We turn now to some brief separate description of them in their contemporary form.

We have already remarked that the Congregational churches have felt more acutely the decline of the last fifty years. In fact traditionally Independency has been characterised by small congregations, and the developments of the later nineteenth century represented a departure from its normal historic form. Indeed, it may be doubted whether a large congregation can know effectively that Christocracy through the church meeting which is at the heart of the Church's origin. We may suspect that not a few of the large Congregational churches of the last generation were governed more by the diaconate than by the church meeting.

Today Congregationalism is a denomination of small churches. With true High Church emphasis the Congregationalists speak in formal documents of 'the church that meets in such-and-such street', rightly identifying the Church with a covenanted fellowship of Christians rather than with bricks and mortar. Nevertheless, in common with many other Free

Churches the congregations find themselves imprisoned in the physical structures of a by-gone age. Few of them compensate for their overwhelming size by either beauty or even seemliness. The material heritage of the Free Churches is almost wholly an encumbrance. Whereas Anglican churches may be overlarge, when rather empty they commonly retain some virtue of worshipfulness. The mass of Free Church buildings inherited from the great chapelbuilding era of Nonconformist expansion had but one virtue; at reasonable expense, such as was possible for an unendowed body of Christians, they held a large number of worshippers within ready hearing of the preaching of the Word, and in sufficient propinquity to one another to encourage the sense of fellowship. When all but empty the preacher finds himself as on a promontory of a pulpit, built to command the now vacant galleries, howling his head off about the intimacies of the Christian religion to a company of people whose fellowship is denied by their being dotted in tiny groups over acres of varnished pitch-pine.

Possibly the crucial question for Congregationalism is whether it can be resolute enough with this cumbersome inheritance, which represents only a passing phrase, and emerge to show the power of a covenanted fellowship of Christians to know Christ as together they seek his will. It is in no danger of a dangerous and atomistic independency. Since 1831 there has been a Congregational Union of England and Wales, and a system of county unions has also grown up. This has been augmented in this century by the appointment of wise and experienced ministers as moderators of large areas, called provinces, who exercise a wholly pastoral function in regard to ministers and congregations within their areas. None of this superstructure, as it were, is possessed of any magisterial power over the churches; but it is possessed of great ministerial influence. Of course, where any financial question enters in, as through the maintenance of the ministry in smaller and poorer churches by the Home Churches Fund, an element of control must of necessity accompany it. Again, while ordination to the ministry of word and sacrament is by the local congregation, with which representatives of the wider Church are normally joined, the Congregational Union will only afford its recognition to men who have received appropriate training for the ministry.

It is important for the members of Churches of a different order to try to understand how the Congregational churches seek to hold independence and fellowship together. As Daniel Jenkins puts it, the congregation 'is independent, not in the sense of walking alone, but in the sense of being an indigenous and self-subsistent centre of Christian life. Possessing all the means of grace, no body on earth can be more fully the church than it.'[1] Congregationalists nevertheless believe that they have a duty to seek fellowship with all other churches, and particularly with those churches holding the same faith and order. Increasingly that fellowship is shown through the Congregational Union of England and Wales, which more and more takes on the appearance of a 'Church' in the sense in which more hierarchical or connexional denominations recognise it. It is a fellowship of mutual caring and counsel rather than a body possessing authority or exercising discipline. If challenged as to what a denomination so ordered can do regarding a congregation, perhaps both minister and people, which had become wayward, the true Congregationalist would have honestly to answer, 'Very little'. But he would count this a price worth paying for the absence of a coercive authority which might more injure the spirit of Christian fellowship than would a few examples of doctrinal eccentricity.[2]

[1] *Congregationalism* (Faber), p. 71.
[2] After all, no Congregational church has in recent years out-paced a former chief Anglican pastor of Birmingham in departure from Christian orthodoxy. We quote this not to score a cheap point, but to emphasise that coercive authority is not lightly used today by any Church, however ordered.

It is striking that any conscious movement within Congregationalism today to give to the Union more the character of a Church is impelled by the desire to facilitate union with other Christians. Congregationalists have not been laggards in the various schemes of union overseas in which they have been involved, and the characteristic modern Congregationalist rather desires that the Congregational emphasis shall not be lost in the Coming Great Church than claims great virtue for a theoretic Independency.

The very heart of the Congregational principle, with its stress upon individual freedom and responsibility in Christ, has forced the Congregational churches into something of eclipse today; but it is not without significance that the British theologian whose work has most strikingly been recovered to challenge and stimulate all the Churches is P. T. Forsyth (1848-1821), a Congregationalist who in his day prophetically warned the churches of his own communion of the perils of a humanistic liberalism. Forsyth's work shows how a truly biblical theology can not only be consonant with Congregational principles, but bear fruit in the whole conception of the Church as a Christ-ruled fellowship, which knows that 'if you work for Christ you are free to adventure in all directions'.[1] The recovery of Forsyth's work, and the recognition that a classic Congregationalism stands for both authority and freedom in an integral relationship, are already leaving their marks on the younger generation of ministers of those churches. Many of them are 'High' Churchmen indeed.

[1] *Peter Taylor Forsyth: Director of Souls,* ed. Harry Escott (Epworth Press), p. 122.

The Baptist Churches

The Baptist churches did not participate in the political struggle of Nonconformity to quite the same degree, although one of their leaders, the redoubtable John Clifford (1836-1923), was both a vehement champion of the working classes from which he had sprung, and a leading protagonist on the Nonconformist side in the fierce conflict over religious education which embittered church relationships in the early part of this century. The Baptists, with their central emphasis upon the need for every man to confess his own personal faith and enter the Church by a baptism which seals his own decision, have understandably stressed the Gospel rather as the Good News which challenges every individual to make the response of faith than as the saving word to society as a whole. This stress has nevertheless imparted a passion for liberty which has often given Baptists, from their origin, a radical approach to politics. But the greatest glory which the English Baptists can claim is that their fellowship nurtured the father of modern missions, William Carey (1761-1834), and therefore pioneered the immense expansion of the Church of Christ throughout the nineteenth century which has made 'the World Church' a living reality to Christians today. The Baptist Missionary Society has a remarkable place in the affection and commitment of Baptist congregations.

It is curious that the Baptist fellowship, which in this way did so much to create the seed-bed of the ecumenical movement, is so ambivalent in its attitude to it. British Baptists have given outstanding leaders to the movement in this day.[1]

Nevertheless it would be disingenuous not to note that

Notably Dr Hugh Martin, one of the chief creators of the British Council of Churches as it is today, and Dr Ernest Payne, who serves as Vice-Chairman of the Central Committee of the World Council of Churches.

there are considerable sections of that fellowship which eye
the whole movement with some suspicion. The ground of tha
suspicion may chiefly be found in the fear that essentia
Evangelical truths may be sacrificed to achieve a superficia
unity. The fears of the Catholic wing of churchmen are bette
known. Those of the Baptists must not be disregarded.

This tension within the Baptist churches corresponds to
a strange paradox about them. They are profoundly suspici
ous of ecclesiasticism. Although the Baptist Union has existe
for almost one hundred and fifty years, and there is a networl
of county associations[1] and superintendents of areas, simila
to the unions and moderators of provinces in Congregationalism, independency is greatly cherished. So great is the
antipathy to anything savouring of priesthood that man
ministers have been 'recognised' rather than ordained, al
though the meaning and practice of ordination are the subjec
of much study at the present time. But with this suspicion o
the ecclesiastical, and indeed of anything that would lesse
the primacy of faith, goes a wonderfully deep commitment to
the Church in her worship and mission. Alone among Britisl
Churches in 'the main stream' of the Christian tradition, Bap
tist churches often see a larger number gathered for worshi
than is in full membership.

It is plain that if the Baptist position on the sacrament fron
which these churches derive their name stresses the individua
response by faith, it simultaneously stresses commitment to
the Christian fellowship. The quality of churchmanship o
many Baptists is striking high, and their pioneering worl
overseas has undoubtedly given them a wider concern for the
Christian mission than most other Churches have. Most congregations in membership of the Baptist Union of Grea
Britain and Ireland will now admit members of other non-
Baptist Churches into membership without demanding tha
they seek believer's baptism, but a great number reserve office

[1] In many cases older than the national Union.

within the Church to those who have entered its fellowship by the sacrament thus practised. Their position is an attempt to practise a comprehensive charity while maintaining their essential witness.

The Baptist churches tend to be more conservative than most in their biblical views, and to practise a definite Puritanism in such matters as consumption of alcohol. Many will be more chary of taking part in various amusements than members of most other Churches. It is probable that as a denomination the Baptists were more widely sympathetic with Dr Billy Graham's campaigns than any other Church. Nor is this surprising when it is recalled that Dr Graham is now a Baptist minister himself.

In worship the Baptists are non-liturgical, as are the other Free Churches. Possibly there remains a greater suspicion of set forms among them than among others. This would be consonant with their history, as will be recalled from an earlier reference. The robed minister, however, is not the rare sight he would once have been, and there is a growing concern for the seemly ordering of worship. As with the Congregationalists, the Holy Communion, or Sacrament of the Lord's Supper, will commonly be observed monthly, or sometimes twice a month, alternately at morning and evening worship. It is still the practice in many Churches for the Sacrament to be an additional service following the customary one. This unhappily suggests that the Communion is a service added by the specially pious to their devotions. There are signs of a change coming here, corresponding to that change in the Church of England which is making the Eucharist the chief service of the day. There is one interesting liturgical practice in the Baptist 'use', in the offering of prayers of thanksgiving for the bread and wine by two appointed deacons. This vocal lay participation is not found normally in the other Free Churches.

Perhaps because of the rather lesser degree in which the

Baptists shared in the struggle of political Nonconformity, they have not suffered as sharp a decline as Congregationalism. Yet again, the very definiteness of the Baptist position has enabled the Baptist churches to hold their own more fully. It is still true that they have shared in the general diminution of Free Church strength, and since as a community the Baptists have been but little drawn from the ranks of the well-to-do, they have felt the economic stresses of recent decades keenly. Smaller congregations have found increasing difficulty in paying their pastors a living wage, and even though their lot has been alleviated in real measure by denominational efforts, the great mass of Baptist ministers know nothing of the affluent society at first hand.

Presbyterianism in England

The Presbyterian Church of England is far smaller than the other so-called main English Free Churches, numbering only some 70,000 members in the whole of the country. Even this membership is found in clusters, chiefly in London, the North East and Merseyside, rather than spread throughout the land. This Church derives little from the historic English Presbyterianism which 'withered away into Arianism'. It is chiefly of Scottish origin although there were elements of the older English Presbyterianism, among those churches which in 1844 formed the independent Church from which the present body directly derives. Although the natural home of the exiled Scot, many of its strongest churches today are in suburbs where they serve as the local Free Church and rely but little on Scottish support.

The significance of this Church in the English scene comes from its representing the great family of Presbyterian and Reformed Churches, and its smallness is a little compensated for by its reflected glory from the northern Establishment. Its worship tends to be more formal than that of the other Free Churches. Robes are *de rigeur* for the minister, who shares not a little of that aura which more markedly surrounds the Scottish than the Nonconformist divine. The demand upon the candidate for the ministry of a degree followed by a full three years of theological study is high (though no higher than that laid upon a candidate for medical practice). The ethos of Presbyterian worship tends to be intellectual rather than emotional. The praise often strikes a Methodist or Baptist as apathetic, and Presbyterian sermons have the reputation of being demanding. These aspects of the Church, together with its common reputation of being the 'Scotch Church', have probably reduced its appeal to working-class people. The rather feline comment of the late Dr W. B. Selbie about Presbyterians that 'their decorous and orderly worship and paternal method of church government serve to commend them in suburban and well-to-do quarters'[1] was probably as true as it was malicious. Its essential truth has little changed in the half-century since he made it; but there has continued to be an indigenous Presbyterianism on Tyneside and in Northumberland as a whole, and a vigorous attempt by the whole Church to take its small place in the Christianising of England. It has worthily resisted the temptation to be an esoteric Church of exiles, and can claim some modest share in the Free Church witness to the nation.

Methodism Today

The Methodist Church, by contrast, is ten times as large, and, while having areas of traditional strength such as Lincolnshire, Cornwall and Durham, is very widespread throughout the land. It is by far the most centralised of all the Free Churches. The individual congregation is part of a circuit, which is led by a superintendent minister, and will according to its size have other ministers on its staff. A number of circuits make up the district. There are thirty-four of these. All the English districts are presided over by a 'separated'

[1] *Nonconformity*, p. 242.

chairman. This office, which only became common a few years ago, is held by a minister who, like a bishop, discharges no other pastoral duties. He is unlike a bishop in not being regarded as different in spiritual office from other ministers, but he is not to be likened to the provincial moderator in Congregationalism or the area superintendent in the Baptist churches. He holds considerable power as the permanent officer of the district synod, and indeed his powers of ministerial discipline (always subject to the synod) make a diocesan bishop's seem small indeed.

Above the districts is the supreme Methodist body—the Conference, over which John Wesley used to preside. The President, a minister elected annually, receives Wesley's Field Bible at his election, and the traditional opening act of praise of the Conference goes back to the earliest days, and recalls the stormy passage which the first preachers had:

> And are we yet alive,
>   And see each other's face?
> Glory and praise to Jesus give
>   For His redeeming grace!
>
> What troubles have we seen,
>   What conflicts have we passed,
> Fightings without, and fears within,
>   Since we assembled last!

Indeed, Methodist history explains much of Methodism. It has today a great deal of the 'feel' of a society, which originally it was. Thus fellowship life is vital to the Methodist. If the Anglican is tempted chiefly to fear today's ecumenical trend for its threat to sound order, and the Baptist for its threat to Evangelical truth, the Methodist is tempted to fear it for its invasion of the warm fellowship which means so much to him.

John Wesley was a travelling preacher, and the Methodist minister today is a travelling preacher too. A circuit may consist of many churches. Many town circuits have country chapels linked to them. While each minister on the circuit will be specially attached to one of the churches, he will throughout each quarter of the year travel about taking services also in the others. In this he and his colleagues will be assisted by some of the nineteen thousand local preachers who are a notable feature of Methodism. While Baptist and Congregational Churches make use of the layman in the pulpit, their use is not on a comparable scale to that of the Methodist Church. The adjective 'local' derives from the original distinction between those preachers who travelled over the country, from whom the present Methodist ministry is derived, and those who, by reason of their occupation, were only available for local duty.

The complex rota of preaching appointments, known as the quarterly plan, is as fundamental a document to Methodism as the term's time-table is to a school. Here again is a point of contrast with the other Free Churches which, whenever there is a minister settled in the pastorate, expect him to be on duty at both services for the great majority of Sundays in the year.

Nor is the Methodist minister's travelling confined to the area of his circuit. The circuit itself in which he serves will be changed frequently. Methodism is singular in the constant and regular movement of its ministers. Normally the first appointment to a circuit is for three years. This may be made as a result of an invitation from a circuit (often given one or two years ahead), or by the direct action of the Stationing Committee of the Conference. Thereafter the invitation may be renewed annually up to six years' service. Then only the special permission of Conference could allow a longer ministry. Thus, while six-year ministries have tended to become more frequent, it will be seen that in a normal ministry of forty years it is likely that a man will have served in about ten different areas. It is not surprising that a Methodist minister will not ask a brother minister 'How long have you been ordained?' but 'How long have you travelled?', and a supernumerary or retired minister will be described in traditional Methodist language as having 'sat down'.[1] The circuit system and an itinerant ministry are unique features of Methodism. There is but little variation in the stipends paid to Methodist ministers, save for small recognitions of seniority and responsibility, and such stipends are described as 'allowances'. The minister is provided with a furnished house by the circuit, as with the frequency of moves he would need to be. There is a very strong brotherly feeling in the ministry of this Church, which possibly derives a good deal from an egalitarian as well as a centralised system.

It is natural with such a mobile ministry that lay responsibility should be strongly developed, even apart from the wide use of the layman as preacher. While Anglican churches build up a natural habit of 'leaving it to the vicar', Methodist churches have to carry more of the load through the laity. This is sheer gain, but there are problems connected with the itinerant and circuit system. There are pastoral achievements which are only possible through a depth of minister-and-people relationship which is not normally achieved in a few years. Again, the great need of today, in a period of near-illiteracy in religious knowledge, is for solid and continuous teaching, such as the many changes of 'the plan' do not readily admit.

This need obviously raises the question of the widespread use of the local preacher. Although local preachers are still a very large company, they are a diminishing one. This is due partly, no doubt, to the decline in church membership itself; and perhaps to the unwillingness of as many as in the past to give themselves to this very demanding ministry. But

---

[1] There is a story of a Methodist minister who, after having 'travelled' for forty years, 'sat down', and had to have his bicycle clips removed under a local anaesthetic. This apocryphal tale links us directly with John Wesley's tireless journeys on his horse.

there cannot but be some question whether such a lay ministry is as acceptable now as it was. The ubiquity of broadcasting has imposed new standards of utterance throughout the country, and the godly rather unlettered preacher of the past cannot hope to win a hearing as readily. Nevertheless it is the local preacher who has made Methodism a national Church. The other Free Churches have tended to be restricted to areas which could maintain a minister for each church (though the Congregationalists and Baptists are now far from achieving this). By the use of local preacher and trained minister combined in the circuit system Methodism attempted and achieved far more. And just as the Presbyterian elder combines an ordinary occupation with ordained office within the Church, so the Methodist local preacher brings to his preaching the testimony of a man who is set in the normal working world.

A notable effort is being made by the Methodist Church to train its local preachers for their large task. A special department provides the means for study, and for guidance which would result in a more continuous ministry being exercised. In certain places a 'team ministry' is used, where the preachers meet and plan their successive acts of preaching in order that effective teaching shall be done. Firm standards for the acceptance and trial of preachers are being insisted upon, and in an exceptionally frank report on *Rural Methodism* presented to the Conference in 1958 the practice of filling up gaps in 'the plan' with preachers from other bodies, often of the 'fringe' type, with no guarantee of their orthodoxy or capacity, was frowned upon.

The gravest problem which Methodism faces—save of course those which it faces in common with all the Churches —is that of redundancy. The earlier divisions in Methodism, combined with an era of cheap labour and materials, produced an excessive zeal in chapel building. The union of 1932 has proved thoroughly successful save in persuading local trustees and congregations to abandon redundant buildings and combine with other 'societies' for more effective work. The attachment to buildings has long survived the attachment to particular branches of Methodism. It results in an appalling waste of ministerial time and material resources. Services and meetings are duplicated and triplicated unnecessarily, and the encouragement which larger numbers could bring to ministers and congregations alike is foolishly denied. Time is doing something to deal with this, but the lament of the inadequacy of what is being done is heard almost year by year in the President's address to the Conference.

This tenderness towards local feeling is perhaps rather creditable in a denomination which is so highly centralised. Few Churches place as much influence in the hands of the secretaries of their departments. The notion—we had almost said 'fiction'—that the President of the Conference is also the chairman of all the Church's Departments results in there being no regular departmental chairmen. This means that the secretaries become very much leaders of the Church. The Presidency is often filled from their ranks, and the ablest among them command much influence. Thus, the General Secretary of the Home Mission Department is quite central in all the evangelistic activity of the Church, and this key position has been held by men of the stature of Dr Luke Wiseman and Dr W. E. Sangster, to name only those not now among us. The Christian Citizenship Department is not only concerned with the struggle against those anti-social influences of liquor consumption and gambling which would be natural for a Church which evangelised an industrial proletariat, but is at work in the whole range of positive and forward-looking concerns for social responsibility and international affairs which the thoughtful Christian citizen should have. Dr Henry Carter, a past General Secretary of that Department, was a pioneer in the work of the Churches for refugees. It is in such departments, staffed most often by men of the first rank in the Church's ministry, that one of the peculiar strengths of Methodism can be seen. Thus its Youth Department has been probably the most active of all in recent years, and it is striking that many of the candidates for the Methodist ministry come today from among those who entered Methodism through its youth clubs from non-churchgoing homes. Methodism has no dearth of candidates for its ministry. (It is this fact that has preserved redundancy from more vigorous attack.)

Because of its many unique features Methodism stands apart from the other Free Churches in many ways; but it is joined with the other Free Churches of both England and Wales in the Free Church Federal Council, which was formed in 1939 by the union of two bodies each with a considerable history. One was a popular movement based on local enthusiasms rather than denominational representation. This was the National Free Church Council, and it had a two-fold concern for co-operation in evangelism and political action to maintain Free Church interests, notably in the education struggle. A good deal later, in 1919, the Federal Council of Evangelical Free Churches was formed on a carefully representative basis, and became what Dr Payne calls 'an increasingly useful clearing-house for matters of common concern, the official as opposed to the free voice of Nonconformity'.[1] It was, however, obvious that the existence of two Free Church bodies was something of an embarrassment, and their later union was unavoidable. It is still doubtful whether their combination is wholly gain. Certainly there is need for a more close-knit expression of the vast amount which the Free Churches have in common than the Free Church Federal Council provides.

For as we come to the close of this chapter, it is the common tradition rather than the many and interesting variations which must rightly be emphasised. It is not only

[1] *The Free Church Tradition in the Life of England*, p. 132.

a common experience of struggle for recognition, or a mutual inability to conform to the national Church which these Churches share. As we said at the beginning, it is basically a certain conviction of the primacy of faith over order, of the central place of the laity in the Church, and of the ministry as serving Christ in the Church rather than creating the Church. These common convictions enable the Free Churches readily to accept a shared ministry in the hospitals and the Forces of the Crown, and to enjoy a mutual recognition of each other's membership. There is, with the small exception of certain Baptist churches, full inter-communion between these Churches. In these ways they show forth what they have together received to preserve for the day when God's diverse gifts shall no longer be distorted by division.

3

THE ROMAN CATHOLIC CHURCH
IN ENGLAND AND WALES

'For the majority of English people there are only two religions,
Roman Catholic, which is wrong, and the rest, which don't
matter.'   *Duff Cooper*, Old Men Forget.

The Appeal of Rome

IN a period of unprecedented and bewildering change the
Chuich of Rome naturally exercises a compelling attraction,
not only for those who by temperament readily seek refuge
from the storm of revolution, but also for those urgent and
questing spirits who more deserve anchorage because they
have deliberately exposed themselves to the heavy seas. The
Roman Church is strangely both accommodating and un-
yielding. The taunt of Hensley Henson that it is 'Judaism,
wondrously interlarded with paganism' possesses considerable measure of truth. She accepts the world in ways which
Protestantism has never felt able to do. She accommodates
herself to elements in human nature which Protestantism
challenges. There is, for example, nothing incongruous to
a Roman priest in raising the funds for a new place of worship by energetically promoting a local football pool. At a
less prosaic level, popular Roman devotions offered in
veneration of, say, a local patron saint in Italy, owe not a
little to ancient Mediterranean paganism. In these things
Rome is not a fastidious mother. Her children may bring
home the oddest objects that they have picked up in the
street.

But then let them be careful how they behave. The
element of attraction in Rome today has not been her lack

of puritan rigour. In regard to those aspects of life in which contemporary men and women have most sought accommodation, such as contraception and divorce, Rome has indeed been utterly adamant. Her attraction has lain rather in a total refusal to be accommodated to the spirit of the age. When everything seems to be being shaken she has sought to manifest herself as that which remains, the infallible, unalterable repository of divine truth, the one Holy Catholic and Apostolic Church, with a life flowing down the centuries since Christ lived upon earth, even if sadly reduced in volume by wayward streams which run out into the sand. Here, after all, is the unmistakeable great Church of the West. It is not to be called the successor to the great undivided Western Church of the Middle Ages, for that would be to suggest a break at the time of the Reformation. This is the same Church, proudly claiming a priesthood tracing its succession back to the Apostle Peter and governed by Popes who claim in literal fact to be his successors in unbroken line as Bishops of Rome, the divinely appointed Vicars of Christ upon earth.

The same paradox as we see here in Rome's combination of accommodation to human nature with total refusal to be accommodated to change appears in another guise in her combination of reactionary suspicion of new 'secular' knowledge with a doctrine of dogmatic development almost breathtaking in its boldness. Thus the attitude of Rome to all the new biblical study which sprang up in the nineteenth century was for long one of fear and condemnation. The Church of Rome is still for all practical purposes fundamentalist. During the identical period the same caution has far from obtained in the field of dogma. Several new dogmas have been proclaimed as necessary for salvation. Among them is the infallibility of the Pope, which was defined at an ecumenical Council in 1870, and, in our own day, the Assumption of the Virgin Mary, defined in 1950. The justification for these bold additions to those beliefs necessary for men's true salvation is given in a doctrine expounded brilliantly by John Henry Newman in his *Essay on the Development of Christian Doctrine*. The central argument is that these things were already present in embryonic or seed form in the scriptural revelation.

Now it is certain that many in this country have been repelled by modern Roman developments of this kind, which seem to lack both sobriety and convincing power. Some of tLem have too much of an air of 'It would be nice to believe this, let us look to see if we can find it in essence in the revelation.' Nevertheless, the intransigence of Rome, her unwillingness to be bludgeoned by a proud human knowledge often too dogmatically asserted, and her bland assertion (as in the definition of the dogma of papal infallibility in the very teeth of nineteenth-century secularism) of unalterable and indestructible powers, has caused her to have a strong appeal in this country. That appeal has been strengthened by the minority position of the Roman Catholic community, which prevented 'Roman fever' from being cured by the chilling spectacle of her power being used, as in countries where she is religiously dominant, to frustrate liberal policies and social betterment. That England is free from anticlericalism even in a day when the Churches are rejected, owes much positively to the dissenting tradition, but negatively it owes much to the absence of Roman Catholic dominance. Where that dominance has been exercised, with the possible single exception of Ireland (where the Roman Church for long symbolised the hopes of an oppressed people) anticlericalism has been widespread.

It is worth while to pause for a moment, before turning to the contemporary situation of Roman Catholicism in England and Wales, to ask why the assertion we have just made should be so. Roman Catholic apologists would doubtless say such opposition is naturally born of the uncompromising, unaccommodating presentation of the faith which their Church makes. Truly there is a rejection and opposition that the proclamation of the Gospel can bring. In that the Church knows the experience of her Master. It is surely not thus that the anticlericalism which makes so much of continental Europe sterile to the seed of the Gospel can be explained. The Church of Rome has in fact believed that she has a right, and indeed a duty, to use the civil power to ensure her position as the one true Church, as she conceives it. The central political question for Roman Catholics in England and Wales during modern times has been the schools issue. She will patently not be content until the total cost of Roman Catholic education, including the provision of new schools, is paid for by public monies. Her claim has a strong appeal to the liberal, democratic mind. Why should not Roman Catholic parents, who pay their due share of rates and taxes, choose how their children should be educated? When, however, we turn to a country such as Spain we find even plain civil rights, such as non-Roman Catholic marriage, denied to the tiny Protestant minorities, and the pressure of the Roman hierarchy exerted to ensure that this situation does not change. When challenged about this the English Roman Catholic will often express regret that in Spain things are so crudely done, but, if well-informed, will be bound to admit that his Church does not admit the claim to freedom to propagate what it regards as error. Thus the appeal here in England to liberal democratic conceptions of fair play is in essence expedient. In a situation of Roman domination, save again possibly in Ireland, the validity of the argument of a parent's right to have his child educated in his own beliefs would not for a moment be admitted if those beliefs were non-Roman.

This last paragraph has not been a diversion into an anti-Papist tirade. Its relevance to our immediate subject is twofold. The education issue is the chief way in which most readers of this book will be asked as citizens to judge the claims of Roman Catholics to fairer treatment; and the same issue focuses in a most practical way the essential difference not only between Romanism and Protestantism, but between Romanism and all other Churches. Many Anglicans are instinctively more attracted to the Church of Rome than to the Free Churches. On this very education issue the Roman Catholic Church and the Church of England have often made common cause to secure more generous grants for denominational schools. In this they have been ranged over against the Free Churches. But it cannot be too strongly emphasised that on the central issue the division is between Rome and the other Churches. The Church of Rome does not believe in education for freedom in the same sense as the other Churches. She believes, indeed, that much of the modern idea of freedom is fundamentally irreligious and secular. Education should be indoctrination, not in the pejorative sense in which the word has come to be used, but a training in the revealed truth, the sound doctrine, taught by an infallible Church. That Church would be failing in her duty of charity if she did not seek to avert the propagation of error or to avoid the exposure of her children to the contamination of falsehood. The Roman Catholic Church has a profoundly different conception from the other Churches of the way God deals with men. With this goes her claim, made not necessarily from pride but from honest conviction, that she alone is the Church, the appointed Ark of Salvation.

It follows from this that Britain is a mission field. Roman Catholic books about the last century in this island are plainly written on this assumption. That Britain is a mission field today for all the Churches will be contended in a later chapter, but this is in a different sense. The Church of England and the Free Churches are at variance at many points, but it is difficult to picture a modern writer of either persuasion writing of inroads into the other tradition's adherents as admirable missionary activity. It is natural for Roman

Catholic writers to do so. It is also right. They would be disguising the true nature of their convictions about the Church if they did any other.

A Mission and its Success

Four dates in the first half of the nineteenth century may be regarded as marking a new beginning for Roman Catholicism in Britain, and determining much of its present character. They are 1829, 1845, 1846-7 and 1850. The first year named was that of Catholic Emancipation. Henceforth the basic civil rights were possessed by English Catholics and gradually they emerged from lives of private obscurity to take their place in public affairs. The year 1845 saw the submission to Rome of the genius of the Tractarian movement, John Henry Newman, after two years lingering on his Anglican death-bed. The large hopes which so distinguished a convert brought to some Roman Catholic leaders were never fulfilled. The stream of Anglican converts did not become a broad river in full spate but remained only a disappointing trickle—and a diminishing one at that. Nevertheless the coming into the Roman Catholic Church of those who had shared the normal privileges of the English upper classes, and notably education in the public schools and ancient universities which provided the normal avenue to power, could not but affect the character of English Roman Catholicism. The contentment of the old Catholic families with an uninvaded obscurity was rudely challenged by the ambitious purposes of a Manning. The same training enabled Manning to make the Archbishop's House at Westminster a natural and continuing point of reference for Whitehall.

It remains true that 1846-7 did more to determine the character of the Roman Catholic Church in Britain than either its emancipation from civil disabilities or its reception of Tractarian converts. The event of these years was neither a political victory nor a spiritual movement; it was a natural disaster—the failure of the potato crop in Ireland. Already in the earlier decades of the century the poverty of Ireland and the increasing industrialisation of the other three countries within the British Isles had caused a steady flow of immigrants. Now it became an almost overwhelming flood. Multitudes of men and women poured over from 'John Bull's other island' to escape death by starvation by seeking a pittance in the quickly-growing industries. In numbers they utterly engulfed the old Catholic families and the group of new English converts. The Irish potato famine determined the character of modern Roman Catholicism in Britain. A Roman Catholic writer asserts that

> the fact that the majority of Catholics in England would henceforward be of a foreign race, loyalty, and way of life would inevitably be a further barrier between a Protestant England and the Church. The Church would appear doubly foreign, Italian in its devotion, Irish in its composition.[1]

The fourth date, 1850, marks the restoration of the Roman Catholic hierarchy. Henceforth English and Welsh Roman Catholics would be under the jurisdiction not of Vicars-General but of prelates bearing such titles as the Archbishop of Westminster. It was a symbol of their emergence from being a tolerated minority with deep memories of hatred and persecution, to a striking measure of confidence. That it might well be over-confidence was illustrated by the 'No Popery' riots which broke out in reaction to the flamboyant pastoral letter 'Outside the Flaminian Gate' sent by Nicholas Wiseman, newly created both Cardinal and Archbishop of Westminster. The ready response, however, to his temperate *Appeal to the British People,* published on his arrival in England, was a truer picture of the tolerance which henceforth was to be extended to his Church. The establishment of the hierarchy marked the full beginning of the Roman Catholic mission to win England.

[1] E. J. Watkin, *Roman Catholicism in England* (OUP), p. 181.

The progress of that mission is extraordinarily difficult to estimate and assess. There are three elements in this difficulty. Reliable statistics are hard to come by, especially for the nineteenth century. Again, the growth in the number of Roman Catholics has to be related to the growth in the total population. Yet again, it is almost impossible to extricate the two main elements from one another; one is the pastoral care of immigrants, chiefly Irish, already Roman in obedience, the other the missionary work which has brought about conversions.

Certainly the care of those already Roman Catholic has been the immediately absorbing work for the Roman hierarchy. Manning wrote in 1882: 'I remember saying that I had "given up working for the people of England to work for the Irish occupation in England".'[1] These waves of immigrants did not settle near the rather isolated Catholic chapels of the old Catholic families, but in the prodigiously growing towns and cities of the new industrial age. The task of providing religious ministrations was a daunting one, and it must be accounted one of the most glorious chapters in the story of British Christianity that it was met. The way in which the Irish immigrants outnumbered the old Catholics can be recognised in Manning's rough estimate that four-fifths of the Catholics in England in 1890 were Irish.[2] This proportion, together with the fact that the settlement was in new areas, indicates the scale on which the work of church extension had to be carried out. When the resolve that all Roman Catholic children should be educated in Roman Catholic schools is added to this need for churches and mass-stations, the task must have seemed formidable indeed. When it is further recognised that the driving force that led to this immigration was destitution to the point of starvation, and

---

[1] Purcell's *Manning*, quoted in *English Catholics 1850-1950*, ed. G. A. Beck (Burns Oates), p. 265.
[2] E. S. Purcell, *Manning*, vol. ii, p. 775.

that the work the immigrants came to was labouring of the most ill-paid kind, the achievement of the period will be seen as almost incredible. Churches were built by the penny contributions of great numbers of dockers, labourers, brick-layers and the like. They were also built on the wonderfully self-sacrificing labour of priests, chiefly Irish, who entirely identified themselves with their almost destitute flocks, and by their heroic toil ensured that in our great cities there were not great colonies of embittered pagans. The desperate situation from which the Irish had fled and the appalling conditions to which they had come drove all too many to find a ready refuge in drink. (So much was this so that a temperance movement arose in the Roman Catholic Church as vehement in its propaganda as any of Puritan origin.) Had their Church failed them at such a time their plight would have been grim indeed. Far from failing, the Church re-sponded to the challenge with amazing power. It may be added that the value of celibacy in the clergy in such an emergency situation was well illustrated.

Professor Denis Gwynn[1] has estimated that in the period 1875-1900 the number of Roman Catholic churches and chapels in England and Wales grew from 1,000 to 1,500. By 1918 this total had increased to 1,900. By the outbreak of the Second World War in 1939 the number had grown to 2,475. In forty years almost a thousand additional places of worship had been erected in England and Wales, and by 1960 there were a further seven hundred.[2] The measure of this growth, as representing a change in the religious situation of the country, is perhaps best recognised by contrast. How many Free Church places of worship have been demolished, or converted into a variety of uses in that period? Observation

[1] See his chapter 'Growth of the Catholic Community', pp. 410-437 in *English Catholics 1850-1950*. I am greatly indebted to this chapter for valuable information.

[2] *Catholic Directory 1960* (Burns Oates), p. 723.

suggests it to be a far greater number than new ones opened.[1]
Obviously the number of places of worship is but a vague
guide to the number of worshippers, but where the trends
are as disparate as this an unmistakeable impression is given
of a highly significant change in the ecclesiastical pattern of
our land.

Again, while the number of Anglican clergy and Free
Church ministers has steadily declined as the twentieth
century has worn on, the number of Roman priests has increased by leaps and bounds. Priests, in England and Wales,
both secular and within the religious orders, probably numbered some 3,000 at the beginning of the century. By 1918
they numbered about 4,000. By 1939 there were 5,600. In
the ensuing decade no less than a further thousand priests
were added, and by 1960 the number had risen to 7,366.[2]
To sum up, there has been a rise of almost 250% in the
manpower available to the Roman Catholic Church in her
mission to England and Wales. The present author has
elicited no more remarkable fact in his examination of the
British Churches today.

The equipment and manpower for such a mission permit
verifiable statistical comparison. It is otherwise with assessment of the size of a religious community, let alone recogni-
zing its constituent parts. Bishop G. A. Beck admits the great
problem here but offered a tentative calculation in 1950 that
whereas between 1911 and 1942 the general population in
England and Wales rose from 36,224,000 to 43,595,000,
the estimated Roman Catholic population rose from
1,793,000 to 2,649,000, a rise from under 5% to over 6%

[1] Confirmation of this general impression can be found in the fact
that the number of Congregational places of worship in England
and Wales fell from 4,666 in 1909 to 2,984 in 1959. (This Church,
however, has suffered probably the greatest loss of membership,
see p. 72).
[2] *Catholic Directory*, p. 723.

of the population.[1] He maintains, further, that such estimates are below the probable size of the Roman Catholic community. Certainly the increase in the number of churches and chapels suggests that they are not exaggerated, for general observation would suggest that the normal Roman place of worship is not underpopulated. 6% may still seem a small proportion of our population, but when the proportion of the population ever to be found within the walls of any church is considered, and the greater proportion of the Roman Catholic community with a regular worshipping habit is remembered, it is a remarkable figure. Protestant Christians would delude themselves if they did not recognise the far greater proportion of Roman Catholics *within the worshipping community today* in comparison with 1900.

There are, doubtless, a number of factors, other than missionary zeal or the intrinsic attraction of the Roman Church, which contribute to this situation. The fact that the great mass of Irish immigrants settled together in certain clearly defined districts made their shepherding much easier. Roughly one-sixth of the whole Irish total was resident in London, and almost an equal proportion in Liverpool and Birkenhead; and about half as many more in Manchester and Salford. The three next centres in importance were Leeds, Bradford and Birmingham. Within these towns and cities there came to be Irish Catholic areas. Their Catholicism, too, was part of their being Irish. There were national and cultural buttresses to religious observance. That the typical Roman priest's ministry was to a relatively unchanging type of area, in a day of otherwise vastly increasing mobility of population, undoubtedly facilitated his effectiveness. If we seem to stress too much the Irish element, we may quote in justification the Roman Catholic writer, Professor Denis Gwynn, who says, 'Any statistical study of the Catholic Church in England

[1] *English Catholics 1850-1950*, p. 587.

and Wales during the past century is . . . largely a study of the Irish immigrants and their descendants'.[1]

Immigration still continues to increase the size of the Roman Catholic community, while certainly doing nothing to give to it a more indigenous aspect. In 1950 there were 92 Polish priests caring for Polish and Central European Catholics who number about 200,000.[2]

Another factor which has undoubtly increased the Roman Catholic proportion of the population has been the firm condemnation of the artificial methods of contraception which would appear to be generally accepted in almost all the rest of the community. There are not lacking signs that that Church is anxious concerning the scale of the laity's apparent disobedience to that teaching. The rising social status of many Roman Catholic families is bringing about a reduction in the size of families generally comparable with that in corresponding non-Roman families. It still remains true that the decline of the birth-rate during this century has been definitely slower in Roman Catholic families.

An apparently adventitious, but surely carefully-planned, rise in Roman Catholic numbers comes about from the effects of the *Ne Temere* decree promulgated in 1908. This enactment requires from the non-Catholic partner in a mixed marriage a solemn undertaking that all the children born of such a marriage shall be brought up within the Roman fold. Without such an undertaking the marriage will not be recognized by the Roman Church.

There remains the most difficult question of all. To what extent has Roman Catholicism grown by directly fulfilling its mission to win England? Even recently the battle has raged on this point between Anglican and Roman spokesmen. Rome has certainly not been hampered by undue reticence in proclaiming her achievements in this field, and certain

[1] *Ibid.*, p. 282.
[2] *Ibid.*, p. 589.

converts, like G. K. Chesterton, have possessed gifts as publicists of singular power. Apart from the period of the Second World War when, interestingly, the number of recorded converts fell steeply, the Roman Church has claimed a rate of conversion of ten to twelve thousand per annum since the 1920's. The previous religious allegiance of these converts is possibly not analysed, or indeed capable of analysis. Professor Gwynn suggests that earlier in this century the decline of the Free Churches provided a harvest of converts. The Church of England continues to supply a very tiny trickle of priests who submit to the Roman claims. It is perhaps not wholly uncharitable to say that their calibre in recent years has not been such as to leave noticeable gaps in Anglican leadership. The fact that Rome appears to exercise less attraction for the abler minds in the Church of England than in earlier generations may be attributed to two factors. The increasing definition of dogmas like the Assumption of the Virgin Mary has been disillusioning to those who feel that doctrines essential to salvation must be related to scriptural revelation. And the wider acceptance of the essentials of the Tractarian position has made the Church of England a happier home for those who would see in her the Catholic Church in England.

Two other elements in the Roman Catholic mission to win England to obedience to the Supreme Pontiff may be briefly identified. From being highly concentrated in certain areas, that Church is now achieving a wider spread throughout the country. The increased mobility of the whole population, the sudden redistributions of the war years, the dispersal of industry, these and other factors have created nuclei of Roman Catholics in many new places. Their spiritual needs afford an opportunity for the establishment of new centres of worship and proclamation of that Church's teaching. There is coming to be a new nation-wide spread.

The other factor is the place of the religious orders, especially in the field of education. Here the resources of the Roman Church, and their flexibility, are remarkable. Considerable sacrifices may be called forth from the Roman Catholic community to find even that small proportion of the cost of a new school which now falls upon it. Once, however, that is found, an invaluable centre has been created in, say, a new town or housing area. To the hall of the school, at minimal expense, a chancel may be added, and a most serviceable church thus created. The religious orders will help to staff the school and immediately the Roman Church is established in strength in a formative period in a new community. The other Churches would do well to consider whether their own strategy and deployment of resources are as adequate to the needs of such areas.

What can Protestants learn?

We have obviously not sought to disguise in this chapter a fundamental disagreement with the Roman Catholic position. To do so would be devious. No Roman Catholic true to his own convictions admires an absence of allegiance by someone else to the truth as he sees it. As a Christian of reformed churchmanship the present author could not but deeply regret if a time should come when the Roman Church as she now is should represent more largely the Christian faith in this land. Truth and charity, however, alike compel us to recognise the large lessons which the non-Roman Churches can learn today from that Church which is the subject of our chapter.

One immense lesson is the absolute centrality of the worship of God through Jesus Christ in the life of the Church. We may reject the doctrine of transubstantiation, or any teaching that the sacrifice of Christ is repeated in the offering of the Mass. We must not reject the example of that Church in showing that it is the Christian believer's plain and simple duty to make a Godward offering of worship in the company of the faithful each Lord's Day. The recognition of this is the very heart of the strength of the Roman Catholic community. The absence of such a recognition is a cardinal weakness of Protestantism.

Another lesson may be expressed as the need to give adequate guidance to the wayfaring Christian man. Again we may reject the way in which Rome seems to keep her children in leading strings, to control their reading, and demand too much their submission to priestly guidance. We may further recognise that this rejection does imply certain plain limitations to the guidance other Churches can give. It remains a question whether in a world in which to seek to be a committed Christian is increasingly difficult the layman cannot reasonably expect from his Church a good deal more definite guidance than he usually gets. A pattern of personal devotional life which a layman can use, a way of seeking spiritual counsel, guiding principles in regard, for example, to reading and entertainment and their effect on the inner life—these are needed by every Christian man today. To be convinced that Rome sometimes gives the wrong guidance or uses wrong ways of asserting her teaching, does not excuse other parts of Christ's Church from doing their duty. Not the least reason why some Christians who are not to be dismissed as merely seeking 'bondage with ease rather than strenuous liberty' make their submission to Rome is that they do not see sufficient effort being made in their own communions to give them the simple direct guidance that they need. This Rome does.[1]

These and other challenges must be accepted. One other which Rome appears to present cannot so readily be regarded as valid. Roman Catholic Churches appear to embrace a

[1] We recall a distinguished gynaecologist of convinced and informed Presbyterian churchmanship who protested that while there was a Protestant outcry against the papal advice about saving the life of the child at the cost of that of the mother, he had received no advice at all from theologians of his Church on this grave issue.

greater variety of social classes than Protestant ones. Certainly the man who earns his living with his hands is more commonly found in the former Church. We may as Protestants admit the impeachment which Harry Emerson Fosdick, the great American preacher, sadly confesses as the greatest grief of his career:

> I note this frustration in trying to save a Protestant congregation from being a class church because it has haunted all my ministry. It constitutes today one of Protestantism's major problems.

But it must, however, be firmly said that the Protestant Churches are attempting something much more demanding than the Roman. This is especially true of Churches of the 'gathered' type. They are, however fumblingly, trying to create a fellowship in Christ of people who are rubbing shoulders with one another, seeking in church meeting and the like to know Christ's will for his Church in that place, and in various forms of common life together are brought into a much closer personal relationship than those of whom their Church chiefly asks that they should be spectators at the priestly offering of the Mass. The measure of failure of the Protestant Churches to transcend the human barriers of education, class and so forth may be lamentable. The measure—even if small—of their success is to be commended. They have faced the test of a full personal encounter in the Christian fellowship.

Again, while it may be true that a higher proportion of men who labour with their hands is to be found in Roman Catholic Churches than in Protestant ones, it is also true that the emphasis upon the performance of specific religious duties rather than the meeting of ethical demands facilitates this. Thus if a Roman Catholic labourer were to get drunk or occasionally blaspheme it is unlikely that his work-mates would taunt him with 'I thought you were a Roman Catholic'. It would be otherwise with a Methodist. No doubt the Puritan

[1] *The Living of These Days* (SCM Press), p. 102.

is always tempted to Pharisaism, mistaking abstention from vice for active virtue. The temptation of the Roman Catholic is not to heed Gladstone's warning, 'Beware lest you make your religion a substitute for your morality.' Thus it may be true that the Roman Church has retained a larger number of those in the slums within her fold. It has partly been by the absence of any rigorous moral challenge.

To sum up, the picture of the Roman Catholic Church in England and Wales is one of a growing and well-equipped Church, deploying increasing resources with enviable strategy. Her appearance, however, is undoubtedly foreign in many ways. As has been stressed throughout this chapter, Romanism is largely the faith of immigrants, chiefly Irish, but also—and notably in recent years—from the continent of Europe. Her church buildings often give colour to the jest about the Church of Rome being 'the Italian mission'. Many do not fit happily into the English scene. Bentley's Westminster Cathedral, for example, reveals an attraction to styles more exotic than Anglicanism has normally sought. Roman Catholicism is, nonetheless, engaged on a conscientious mission to this land. Her appeal is that of a dogmatism which yields to nothing, and indeed puts forth new and startling branches. Her challenge to the other Churches is to find whether they can achieve a like commitment to mission without abandoning either their respect for the freedom of the individual will, which is at least a part of essential Protestantism, or their readiness to believe that God may speak through man's discovery of new knowledge.

4

THE SCOTTISH CHURCHES

'Our history is a long one; we go back beyond the Disruption,
the Relief, the Secession; back beyond the Revolution Settlement
and the Scottish Reformation, in which we are proud to claim
our portion; back by way of Iona, guided by the light of St
Kentigern and the Candida Casa of St Ninian, even unto
Jerusalem.' *John White,* Moderator, at the union General
Assembly of the Church of Scotland, 1929.

The Church of Scotland

THE Scottish people seems irrevocably Presbyterian. Amid
so much in these chapters which has to be hedged about
with qualifications, it is a relief to be able to make so firm
and unequivocal a statement. It is true that there is one other
sizeable Church in Scotland—the Roman Catholic. But, as
in England, that Church is composed, as to the vast majority
of its adherents, of Irish immigrants. There are over
1,300,000 communicant members of the Church of Scotland.
Four other Churches, which are small but also Presbyterian
in polity, number between them well over 50,000 communicants. The largest Church in Scotland which is neither
Presbyterian nor Roman Catholic is the Episcopal Church
(Anglican) which comprises only some 56,000 communicants. Congregationalism numbers around 35,000 members,
the Baptists some 20,000, and the Methodists less than
14,000. Apart from the immigrant Irish, largely settled in
Glasgow and the industrial belt of the Clyde Valley, the
inhabitants of Scotland are overwhelmingly Presbyterian.

The Church of Scotland is unique in a number of ways. It
is the only British Presbyterian Church which enjoys national
recognition. (It is amusing to find the lengths to which

Anglo-Catholic journals will go to avoid using the proper name of this Church. 'The Presbyterian Church of Scotland' is one unhappy solecism. The alternative seems to be to refer to 'the Kirk' in a rather jocose fashion. Anything will serve rather than the admission that it is what it claims to be, the national Church of Scotland.) Again, it cannot accurately be described as a 'State' Church, and only in a rather loose sense since 1921 as an 'established' Church. Both phrases imply an element of subordination to, or even creation by, the State. In 1921 an Act of Parliament recognized the important 'Articles Declaratory of the Constitution of the Church of Scotland on Matters Spiritual'. This declaration by the Church of Scotland, as it then was, was an essential step in preparation for the creation of the Church of Scotland as it is today. The Church took its present form by the union of the Church of Scotland with the United Free Church in 1929. The 'Articles Declaratory' make this firm and characteristically Calvinist affirmation concerning the sovereignty of Christ over his Church:

> IV. The Lord Jesus Christ, as King and Head of His Church, hath therein appointed a government in the hands of church office-bearers, distinct from and not subordinate in its own province to civil government. The Church of Scotland, while acknowledging the Divine appointment and authority of the civil magistrate within his own sphere, and holding that the nation acting in its corporate capacity ought to render homage to God and promote in all appropriate ways the interests of His Kingdom, declares that it receives from its Head and from Him alone the right and power subject to no civil authority to legislate, and to adjudicate finally, in all matters of doctrine, worship, government, and discipline in the Church ...

This position is in sharp contrast with that of the southern establishment. The Church of England is, as the law stands at present, subject either to Parliament or the Judicial Committee of the Privy Council in regard to doctrine, worship, government and discipline. Knowing this, an Englishman may wonder in what sense the Church of Scotland, with this firm declaration of absolute spiritual autonomy, can claim to be national. In fact the Treaty of Union in 1707 made provision for the security of the Church of Scotland, and to this day the first oath which the Sovereign makes on accession is to preserve that Church. The same 'Articles Declaratory' of 1921, moreover, make plain the Church's understanding of both its national status and the duties which that implies. The later part of Article III runs:

> *As national* it is a representative witness to the Christian faith of the Scottish people, and acknowledges its divine call and duty to bring the ordinances of religion to the people in every parish of Scotland through a territorial ministry.

A Presbyterian Church is a Church possessed of a certain form of government; that is, government by presbytery, as an episcopal Church is governed by bishops. The distinction is, of course, doctrinal as well as ecclesiastical. The Church of Scotland follows the classic Presbyterian model which is briefly outlined in the earlier chapter on the English Free Churches. The Kirk Session is the court for each congregation, presided over by the minister, and consisting of the elders, who in Scotland are men[1] ordained to spiritual office for life as ruling elders. The Presbytery is the regional court, meeting perhaps monthly and consisting of the ministers of the parishes within the area, together with a representative elder from each congregation. The Presbytery is charged with the full *episcopé,* or oversight, of the Church within its bounds, in the same way as the bishop is related to his diocese in an episcopal Church. Thus, for example, while the minister is elected by the congregation, each election is subject to the approval of the Presbytery, and once the minister has been

---

[1] Women, being ineligible for ordination to either the ministry or eldership, are excluded from the government of the Church of Scotland.

inducted to the charge of that parish he is subject to the discipline of the Presbytery, not of the congregation. His 'parson's freehold' is in effect as secure as that of any Anglican incumbent. The Presbyteries within a wider area are joined in Synods, but these bodies play a less direct and influential part than the other courts. The supreme court of the Church of Scotland is the General Assembly which meets in May for almost two weeks in the Assembly Hall in Edinburgh. The Assembly consists of representative ministers and elders, in equal numbers from the whole Church, chosen normally by rota on a presbytery basis.

One further unique aspect of the Church of Scotland, in addition to those which have already been mentioned, is that it is in the strange position of being the national Church of a nation that has no separate existence as a State. One effect of this is to give the General Assembly the status not only of the supreme court of the Church but also of something of a national forum. The panoply of pageantry which attends the parliament of a Church otherwise noted more for its austerity than its flamboyance emphasises this impression. The Queen appoints her Lord High Commissioner to attend the Assembly. He takes up residence in the Palace of Holyroodhouse and drives in state each morning to the Assembly, of which, however, he is not a member. So rigid is the symbolism of a national recognition which implies no authority that the Lord High Commissioner must reach his gallery without passing through the Assembly. Collectors of the significant anecdote will find an admirable specimen in the life of John White, the architect of the reunion of the Scottish Church. When the Duke of York (later King George VI) was to attend the union Assembly of 1929 an over-zealous equerry, Admiral Sir Basil Brooke, was insistent that the Duke, as Lord High Commissioner, must enter through the Assembly. Dr White's reaction was peremptory. It was 'to state in unmistakeable terms that, if the Admiral . . . did not

agree, they could have no Lord High Commissioner present.'[1]
The Duke himself saw the point immediately.

There is a great deal of Scottish church history in that
seemingly trivial incident. Nothing, indeed, could have more
marred the great act of reunion of the two large Scottish
Churches than even a ceremonial suggestion that the State
could interfere with the life of the Church of Jesus Christ.
Although in this brief chapter we can do little to trace the
history of the Church in Scotland, we must describe sufficient
of it to explain the unique character of the Church of Scotland
today of which we have spoken.

As we write, the fourth centenary of the Scottish Reformation in 1560 has just been celebrated with considerable
ceremony, including the presence of Her Majesty the Queen
in person rather than represented by her Lord High Commissioner. The climacteric event of 1560 did not, of course,
happen out of the blue. The preceding decades had seen many
signs of the weakening of Scottish ties with the Papacy, and
the ferment of the Reformers' ideas had been at work north
as well as south of the Border. 1559 saw the return to Scotland of John Knox, who had been preaching Protestant ideas
at St Andrews when the castle, held by a body of Protestants,
was in turn taken in 1547 by France. Knox was condemned
to eighteen months' service as a galley-slave. This terrible
experience, as well as ruining his health, gave him a lasting
bitterness against Catholic France. The succeeding years
were with but a year's exception, 1555-6, spent outside
Scotland. During part of the time he was in England, being
chaplain to Edward VI and assisting Cranmer in the revision
of the Second Prayer Book. At this time he gained a great
love for Protestant England. Then for three years he was the
pastor of the English Church at Geneva and drank deeply of
the waters of Calvinism at their very fountain-head.

Thus when he returned in 1559 to his native land he was

[1] Augustus Muir, *John White* (Hodder & Stoughton), p. 263.

not only confirmed in his earlier Protestantism, but was determined to turn Scotland from her hereditary ally, Catholic France, towards her traditional enemy, Protestant England.

His vehement preaching won an immense response, and in 1560 the foundation stones of the Scottish Reformation were laid. 'In August Parliament ended the authority of the Pope in Scotland, adopted a reformed Confession of Faith and forbade the celebration of the Mass.' Possibly more than anything else, this Reformation was a revolt for pastoral reasons. That the hungry sheep looked up and were not fed was the plain truth about the Church in Scotland at that time. The wealth and resources of the Church were in the hands of the hierarchy and the monasteries, and the provision for the parishes was appallingly meagre. That ministry which obviously should be basic, the care of souls in the places where men live, was disregarded. The Reformers set their hands to an entire upturning of this ludicrous situation. It is a Scottish Episcopalian who has written:

> The Reformation was in any event anti-monastic, and it was critical of cathedrals and collegiate churches, monuments as they were to the neglect of the cure of souls. If, then, the monasteries, friaries and collegiate churches were stripped of their wealth, and the parishes regained the revenues which properly belonged to them, a competent ministry could be maintained throughout the land, ministers and their flocks could be educated, churches could be decently maintained.[1]

The modern tourist looking at the great ruined cathedral at St Andrews, or the lovely remains of the abbeys at Melrose and Dryburgh, may lament the iconoclasm of the Reformers. Their concern, however, was not with the eventual gratification of the sightseer, but with the application of the resources of the Church to their primary purpose, making Christ known and loved by the people of the land. The great

[1] Gordon Donaldson, *Scotland: Church and Nation through Sixteen Centuries* (SCM Press), pp. 54-5.

monastic buildings fell into disrepair because there was no longer any use for them.

The parochial ministry has continued to be central in the Church of Scotland. That Church looks today with suspicion on any use of ministers outside the parochial system, and some, at least, of the doubts with which many have regarded the Iona Community founded by Dr George MacLeod have been due to its creation of a loyalty beyond the parish other than to the higher Church Courts.

The Scottish Reformation, as we have said earlier when contrasting it with that in England, was thorough-going and drastic. While, due to the changes of policies, it was 1690 before the office of bishop fully disappeared, and Knox indeed desired the use of superintendents, this was a Presbyterian reformation. This meant that the priest was replaced by the minister of word and sacraments. With the priests' disappearance came a new place for the laity, especially expressed through the office of the eldership, of which we have written in an earlier chapter.

But it was not only that the laity, through the eldership, came to have a quite new place in the government of the Church. Worship, too, became not a priestly act but the work of the whole *laos,* the people of God. The Holy Communion could not, as Calvin had vainly wished at Geneva, become the normal Sunday by Sunday service, for mediaeval Catholicism had accustomed people to communicating but once a year, but when it was observed the laity communicated in both elements and gathered around the table which was often placed down the aisle. What has remained a noted part of Scottish worship (as, indeed, it was for long part of English worship) was now introduced—the psalter in metre. Often uncouth, though sometimes achieving a spare and rugged beauty, and commonly linked to noble tunes, the metrical psalms have become part of the very stuff of Scottish history. One other feature introduced at this time is totally unknown today. Service-books were set in the hands of the congregation, and it may well have startled some who celebrated the fourth centenary of the Reformation, and who would greet their own minister's introduction of a simple response with 'It's no' Presbyterian', to learn that part of what they celebrated was the introduction of liturgical books to the congregation. It is today a paradoxical fact that the Church which most radically rejected a priestly ministry is content to have the whole of the people's offering of worship to God, save for the hymns or psalms, made by the minister.

Nevertheless the worship of the Scottish Church today is far richer than it was for centuries. Knox's Book of Common Order did not hold sway for long, and the influence of English Puritanism added to a rigorous Calvinism tended to make the preaching of the Word all, and the offering of worship meagre and thin. This is sometimes misunderstood by those who stand in the 'Catholic' tradition in a disturbing way. They imagine that what man said mattered, and the Godward side was forgotten. The original motive for this imbalance was entirely otherwise. There was a horror of man pretending to offer God worship through mere creaturely objects—as the mediaeval Church had done. What God spoke to men through the right dividing of his Word was necessarily central in worship. The tendency of Calvinism is always to begin not where men are, but where they ought to be. The sovereignty of God must so be set forth that man is moved to awe not by the devices of architects and ecclesiastical furnishers but by the prophetic 'Thus saith the Lord'. The danger of Scottish worship was not that it forgot God that man's voice might be heard, but that in its emphasis upon the transcendance of God it forgot man in his actual frailty. The priesthood of all believers was a great emphasis of the Reformers, but the people's priestly offering of worship tended to be over-shadowed by the dominance of the prophetic word. Today, although the preaching of the Word still has central place in the worship of the Church of Scotland, the other acts of worship are richer and more carefully ordered. *The Book of Common Order* published in 1940, and *Prayers for the Christian Year,* official though wholly optional publications of the Church of Scotland, both mark the effect of the work of those who pioneered a return to the tradition of Knox. They have set a standard for worship of great influence.

The Divisions of Presbyterianism

It was not John Knox but Andrew Melville (1545-1622) who fully worked out the doctrine of 'the two Kingdoms' which finds reflection in the Articles Declaratory of the Church of Scotland today. ('The Lord Jesus Christ, as King and Head of the Church, hath therein appointed a government ... distinct from and not subordinate in its own province to civil government.') Knox, like his master Calvin, thought of Church and State being one, not of course in an Erastian sense but a theocratic one. It was the continuing political struggle and the obduracy of the Stuarts which forced Melville to establish a more thorough-going Presbyterianism, in which the General Assembly was not, as in Knox's day, formed of 'the three estates', barons, burgesses and clergy, who sat in the Scottish Parliament, but a wholly ecclesiastical body made up of ministers and elders chosen by the Church.

Since Melville's day the idea of the two Kingdoms has been an integral part of what Scotland understands by the Reformation. It was this conception which underlay the greatest and most heroic of the many complex divisions of Scottish Presbyterianism. In 1843, after a long and vain struggle to rid the Church of Scotland of lay patronage, 451 ministers led by Thomas Chalmers forsook all the securities of an established Church, stipends, manses and glebe-lands, in testimony that Jesus Christ must be King and Head of his Church. This act—the Disruption—must be deemed one of the most heroic in British church history. This was in fact the great price with which the Church of Scotland today obtained its freedom. Those south of the Border who are envious of that may rightly consider whether there have not been points in English church history when a like sacrifice was refused. The Free Church of Scotland existed separately but for fifty-seven years, for in 1900 it united with the United Presbyterian Church, itself the product of an earlier union of separated Presbyterians, to form the United Free Church. This Church in turn had but twenty-nine years of life, for all but a small part of it, which still continues a separate existence, united in 1929 with the 'Auld Kirk', the Church of Scotland as it then was.

The little more than half century of the Free Church's separate existence saw an amazing flowering of Christian generosity and enterprise. Theological colleges which rapidly achieved the highest reputation were established at Aberdeen, Edinburgh and Glasgow, and a great foreign missionary work was begun. All this was done while church buildings had to be provided throughout the land, manses had to be built, and the maintenance of the ministry had to be achieved wholly from voluntary offerings. In a few decades a Church was formed which, especially after the union with the United Presbyterian Church in 1901, could in every regard stand comparison with the ancient established Church of the land. Not that that Church remained as barren as might have been feared in 1843 when the vast majority of the most Evangelical and the most courageous ministers went forth in faith at the Disruption. As Sir Charles Petrie has remarked,

When the lapse of a few years had enabled the situation to be regarded more objectively it was found that the Church, though greatly diminished in strength, was not as moribund as its critics were led to believe.[1]

[1] *The Victorians* (Eyre & Spotiswoode), p. 147. If Norman MacLeod of the Barony, Glasgow (grandfather of Dr George MacLeod), was a giant and untypical, it must still be recognized that such a

The tragedy of the Disruption was chiefly to be found in the Highlands and Islands, where the great majority adhered to the Free Church.

The grim legacy of Presbyterian division is still there, where sparsity of population makes it the more appalling. The Disruption caused two churches to be established in many parishes of tiny population. Then in 1893 a splinter Church—called the Free Presbyterian Church—came into existence, claiming to be the true heir of the Church of the Disruption on the ground that in the previous year the Free Church of Scotland by making more liberal its adherence to the Westminster Confession of Faith (the classic document of British Presbyterianism) had denied its own continuity. This little Church numbers a total community of some five thousand, of whom only a small proportion are communicant members. (In the Highlands a strong tradition remains of unwillingness to be committed to communicant membership for fear of unworthiness.) Yet again, when the Free Church united with the United Presbyterian Church in 1900 there was a dissident group in the Highlands and Islands which claimed to be the true continuing Free Church, in that that Church at its origin was committed to belief in the principle of establishment (while maintaining that the form of it was wrong), and therefore could not unite with Presbyterians who held the voluntary principle. This small body, the present Free Church of Scotland, actually won from the House of Lords a declaration that it was the true heir and successor of the Disruption Church and received all the immense property of that Church—an odd decision that had rapidly to be substantially reversed by an Act of Parliament. It is this little Church which is the most widely known of the small Presbyterian bodies, generally under the nickname 'the Wee

man deliberately chose to stay in the Auld Kirk. See *Fathers of the Kirk* (OUP), a most attractive recent compendium of short biographies of Scottish church leaders.

Frees' (as contrasted, that is, with the great Free Church of Scotland within which they were a dissident group). Its fifteen Presbyteries are chiefly groupings of Highland and Island charges. Its membership is round about six thousand, although, like the Free Presbyterians, the 'Wee Frees' have a larger community, perhaps numbering some 25,000. Its tiny size may well be remembered by those who read its strictures on, say, the Royal Family's Sunday occupations. Such readers are sometimes apt to identify their attitudes with those of all Presbyterians in Scotland.

The only remaining Presbyterian Church of any size is formed of that part of the United Free Church which chose not to enter the union of 1929. It has a communicant membership of some 24,000. It believes in total separation of Church and State and wholly voluntary support of the Church, but is contrasted with the other small Presbyterian groupings in marked ways. Whereas the others are intensely conservative, and indeed are of historical interest as preserving aspects of Scottish Presbyterianism from which the main body of the Church has now departed, the United Free Church is avowedly liberal and 'progressive'. Alone among Scottish Presbyterian Churches it opens all offices, including the eldership and the ministry, to women. Further, it alone opens the moderatorship of both Presbytery and Assembly to elders. On most social questions this Church takes a very liberal view. Again by contrast with the other small Churches, its strength is in the Lowlands and cities.

This brief description of three other Presbyterian Churches in Scotland leads us to emphasize again the overwhelming position of the Church of Scotland numerically, and the fact that while there has been massive dissent from the national Church its character in the past was wholly different from that in England, and its size at the present is almost minute. Hensley Henson has perceptively expressed the contrast with England:

Dissidence has been as conspicuous in Scotland as in England, but in Scotland there has been nothing properly equivalent to English Dissent. Separations within the common Presbyterian description have been many north of the Tweed, but not dissenting denominations organising their systems according to their own will. The Westminster Confession and the Presbyterian polity have held Scottish Christians in a fundamental agreement, but between the English Dissenters and the Established Church there are no such strong and recognised links.[1]

Presbyterianism in Scotland has certainly proved fissiparous. It is easier to erect a dissenting Presbytery than to consecrate a schismatic bishop, and the tendency in Presbyterianism, certainly when held by Scotsmen, is to prize purity of doctrine or ecclesiastical freedom more than unity. But the year 1929 saw the restoration of much that had been lost by this tendency. The great union of that year brought together all but a few tens of thousands of the Presbyterian family in Scotland. Humanly speaking its architect was John White of the Barony, Glasgow. It was he who led his own Church—the 'Auld Kirk'—to remove the remaining stumblingblocks to union, chiefly the mode of tenure of property, and the last vestiges of state authority within the Church. Tireless in negotiation, adamant on principle, and ruthless in dealing with timorous governmental authorities, he sought with unremitting ardour the creation of a Church which should be both fully national yet wholly free. Nothing short of organic union would do. Even as far back as 1907 he declared that the way of co-operation was wholly inadequate, and that a full corporate union must be their goal. Twenty two years later he saw his dream fulfilled.

Looking at the Church of Scotland as it it today, the observer is tempted to feel that it is as though the United Free Church had never been. The present temper of the Church is intensely national, and even somewhat selfconsciously Scottish. It is indeed a very large Church in a small nation.

[1] *The Church of England,* pp. 50-51.

The characteristic radical emphases of the United Free Church seem little in evidence. Yet Dr Gordon Donaldson's words must be weighed as a corrective to this impression:

> It is plain that, so far from the Free Church and the United Presbyterian Church having compromised their principles by entering into union with the Church of Scotland, it was the latter which had conceded almost everything for which the Seceders and the founders of the Free Church had contended.[1]

Probably more has been done in Scotland than in reunited Methodism to eliminate the redundancy which the duplication of schism creates. By 1960 there had been 783 local unions of churches, with, in addition, 105 linkings. The firmness with which this has been done has been compelled not a little by the increasing scarcity of ministers to staff unnecessary churches. But there has been a wonderful growing together of the different traditions represented in that union which is now over thirty years old. Today the great majority of ministers have been ordained into the reunited Church, and the old distinctions are being rapidly effaced.

Nowhere has this unity been of more gain than in the work of national church extension. Both the increase in the Scottish population and the creation of new towns and vast new buildings estates challenge that Church which, in words already quoted, 'acknowledges its divine call and duty to bring the ordinances of religion to the people in every parish of Scotland through a territorial ministry'. In this work, too, John White was the great leader. Its success, and the ability which the church extension charges have shown to gather in some part of that section of the population most alienated from the Church, derive chiefly from their being representative of the one national Church.

[1] *Scotland: Church and Nation*, p. 102.

Other Scottish Churches

When we turn to the non-Presbyterian Churches we need again to remind ourselves of the paucity of their numbers (other than in the Roman Catholic Church). Thus Methodism, while in the British Isles the third largest non-Roman Church, is sparsely represented in Scotland, where John Wesley scattered seed which proved to fall on stony ground in terms of fruit in specifically Methodist societies. Scottish Congregationalism represents a union of Congregational churches with the Evangelical Union in 1896 and can rightly claim to be an indigenous growth and not an importation from England. The Baptist Union of Scotland consists largely of small churches, outside the cities more strongly represented on the east coast than elsewhere. The churches which comprise the Union tend to be conservatively Evangelical, and the Union has the unhappy distinction of being the first Church to withdraw by deliberate act from the World Council of Churches. (It retains its membership in the British Council.)

One other Church, although it is but the size of the Baptist and Congregational Churches combined, demands fuller treatment both for historical and contemporary reasons. That is the Episcopal Church in Scotland. It is commonly called 'the English Church'; being indeed a sister Church of the Church of England and the rightful spiritual home of Englishmen of Anglican churchmanship when they reside in or visit Scotland. Once again, however, it can claim to be an indigenous growth, and takes its separate form from the final rejection of episcopacy by the national Church in 1690. The eighteenth century was a period of disunity, with some Episcopalians accepting the Revolutionary Settlement of 1688, and others taking a 'non-juring' Jacobite line. Although the latter body suffered terribly from governmental persecution, and was thereby greatly diminished in numbers, it had

the remarkable privilege in 1784 of consecrating the first
bishop for the now independent colonies in America. Thus
the great Protestant Episcopal Church in the USA has episcopal orders which spring from the tiny and persecuted
Church in Scotland. The death of the Young Pretender
in 1788 opened the way for reconciliation between the
nonjuring Episcopalians (who were now ready to accept
the Hanoverian succession) and those who worshipped
in the 'qualified chapels', which used the liturgy of the
Church of England and were under the authority of English
bishops.

In 1811 a synod was convened by the bishops and declared
to be the National Synod of the Episcopal Church in Scotland. Throughout the nineteenth century the development of
the Church was to bring it more into line with the Church
of England than the Scottish episcopalianism of the past, and
also to accept in somewhat wholesale fashion the innovations
of the Tractarians. The ritual is perhaps as advanced as any to
be found in the Anglican Communion. Today two Prayer
Books are used side by side—the Book of Common Prayer
of the Church of England and the Scottish Prayer Book, last
revised in 1929. While the laity share in the election of a
bishop, and sit in the Consultative Council and in the Representative Church Council (whose function is wholly
financial), they are excluded from other executive aspects of
the Church's government. This contrasts sharply with the
position in the two disestablished Anglican Churches in Ireland and Wales, and is possibly a reaction against the
Church of Scotland's use of the elder in parity with the
minister throughout its government.

Bishop Stephen Neill comments on this Church:

Existing as a small minority Church (not more than five per cent
of the population) . . . the Scottish Church exhibits both the merits
and defects of minorities; on the one hand great devotion, on the
other, a certain narrowness of outlook and a defensive mentality,

on which participation in the wider life of the Anglican communion, and of the ecumenical movement, is having a widening and mellowing effect.[1]

In view of the recent conversations between Anglican and Presbyterian Churches north and south of the Border, it is perhaps regrettable that the Church of Scotland sees Anglicanism most closely in one particular form. The large claims of the Episcopal Church and the high-sounding territorial titles of her six bishops accord strangely to Scottish Presbyterian ears with her actual size, but this small Church is passionately convinced that it represents the continuing true Church of Scotland. The outside observer can recognise the contribution which an Anglican Church has to make to Scottish Christianity, and can but hope that the ecumenical forces within that Church may come to have such strength that that contribution may be offered without some of its less fortunate concomitants. It is only honest to recognise that often the Episcopal Church is that of the laird, or of that part of local society which has been educated at English public schools. Thus a regrettable 'sociological factor' enters in here to affect church relationships. Yet again, at times the little Episcopal Church has felt that her large sister south of the Border was ready to treat with the Church of Scotland with insufficient recognition that a common churchmanship should be a closer tie than a shared national status. Certainly the Episcopal Church in Scotland could play a very large part in easing the way to closer relationships between all Anglicans and Presbyterians, and bears faithful witness to elements in the Christian tradition which the more rigorous Scottish Reformation long neglected.

[1] *Anglicanism* (Pelican), p. 282.

The Roman Catholics

Before we close this chapter we should note the great strength of the Roman Catholic Church in the city of Glasgow and the area of heavy industry in its environs. It has been possible to leave it on one side in considering the ecclesiastical life of the Scottish people, for the reason given at the beginning of our chapter. It is very much a Church of the immigrant Irish. Unlike England, Scotland had few Roman Catholics after the Reformation, although 'there was in certain regions what has been called a "Catholic interest", politically conservative, allergic to the ethos of the New Religion but in the last resort singularly indeterminate'.[1] At the end of the seventeenth and during the early eighteenth century many families in the Highlands were won for the Roman Church, but as in England and Wales the growth of that Church to any significance dates from the great nineteenth-century immigration of Irish Catholics, coming to escape starvation in the rapidly growing industry of the Clyde Valley and beyond. The hierarchy was established in 1878. It is estimated that in 1893 the Roman Catholic population (not to be confused with a *membership* figure like that of the Church of Scotland) in the Archdiocese of Glasgow was 250,000, served by some 150 priests. By 1947 it had doubled and, even more significant, was served by 500 priests.[2] During the following year the Archdiocese (which had embraced the City of Glasgow, N. Ayrshire, the Cumbrae Isles, Dunbartonshire, Lanarkshire and Renfrewshire) was divided into three, forming the province of Glasgow, by the creation of suffragan sees at Paisley and Motherwell. Although there is another

[1] David Mathew, *Scotland under Charles I,* p. 20, quoted by Donaldson, *op cit.,* p. 108.
[2] See John Highet, *The Churches in Scotland Today* (Jackson), pp. 35-36. The same author's later book, published in 1960, *The Scottish Churches* (Skeffington), gives an interesting picture of contemporary Scottish church life and activity.

province, of which the Archbishop of St Andrews and Edinburgh is the Metropolitan, the numerical strength is concentrated in the western Lowlands.

The fact that the Roman Catholic Church is chiefly Irish
in composition, working-class in character, and highly concentrated in certain areas, has led at times to clashes, chiefly
in Glasgow, largely social in origin, but religious in colour.
The tensions which such clashes express probably have some
effect upon Presbyterians in making them more fiercely
opposed to any change which can be regarded, however in-
accurately, as involving a danger of 'Popery'.

Unity and the Future

It is singularly difficult for Englishmen to recognise the
degree to which in Scottish history religious and ecclesiastical
questions have been interwoven with the central issues of the
national life. While, as we have seen in earlier chapters, in
England, too, religious questions have emerged to play a not
inconsiderable part in our story, they have not continued to
be 'live' to the present day. In Scotland they have. Thus if
English people have been startled by the storm and fury to
which 'the Bishops Report' (i.e., the report on Anglican-
Presbyterian conversations published in April 1957[1]) gave
rise in Scotland, in Scotland they have been appalled at the
indifference of the English churchman to so remarkable a
document. There is in Scotland a far longer and continuing
tradition of theological debate at the popular level. Future
attempts to advance the cause of Christian unity there must
take more serious account of this. Whatever the defects of
the Presbyterianism which, as we have seen, has dominated
and still dominates the Scottish religious scene, it has not
failed to produce a responsible and instructed laity. Before
such a laity a compelling vision of the unity of the Church

[1] *Relations between Anglican and Presbyterian Churches: a Joint
Report* (SPCK).

must be set, before the necessary disturbance of customary ways will be faced by a Church already so strong in numbers and so deeply embedded in the national life.

5

THE IRISH PROTESTANT CHURCHES

> There in pinnacled protection
> One extinguished family waits
> A Church of Ireland resurrection
> By the broken, rusty gates.
>
> *John Betjeman*, Sunday in Ireland.

The Church of Ireland

THE susceptibilities of Catholic-minded Anglicans are readily offended by the word 'Protestant'. This sensitiveness drives an author to such unhappy negative descriptions as 'non-Roman'. In speaking, however, of the Churches of Ireland[1] other than the Roman Catholic, the word 'Protestant' can be used without offence. The Church of Ireland—sister Church of the Church of England—normally glories in her Protestantism. The only other Protestant Churches of any size are the Presbyterian Church in Ireland and the Methodist Church in Ireland. There is a Non-subscribing Presbyterian Church allied to the English Unitarian Churches—but it has a small membership. The independent Churches, whether Congregational or Baptist, have never established themselves in any strength in Ireland. In Belfast most notably, but also in other parts of Northern Ireland, the mission halls of a fundamentalist and revivalist character are both far more numerous and far better attended than elsewhere in the United Kingdom. They form a marked feature of Ulster religious life, however it may be interpreted.

---

[1] The word 'British' in our title suggests we should limit ourselves to Northern Ireland, but the Churches are not divided between the Province and the Republic. We only treat of the Roman Catholic Church—so dominant in the Republic—insofar as it impinges on the other Churches.

It is perhaps not too exaggerated a form of historical short-hand to say that the Reformation never really happened in Ireland. True, the Papal Supremacy was abolished, but this, as G. M. Trevelyan remarks, 'had always remained a some-what alien power' to the Celt. The monasteries too were dissolved. But these were negative acts. Nothing was provided to fill the vacuum, for the English Bible and the English Book of Common Prayer were unintelligible to the Irish-speaking peasant. In the days of Elizabeth a policy of Pro-testant colonisation was followed. Dr Trevelyan with masterly succinctness has summed up the effects of this in a single paragraph which provides the clue to the succeeding centuries of Irish religious history:

> And so, in the last thirty years of Elizabeth's reign, Irish history, till then fluid, ran into the mould where it hardened for three hundred years. The native population conceived a novel enthu-siasm for the Roman religion, which they identified with a passionate hatred of the English. On the other hand the new colonists, as distinguished from the old Anglo-Irish nobility, identified Protestantism with their own racial ascendancy, to maintain which they regarded as a solemn duty to England and to God. Ireland has ever since remained the most religious part of the British Islands.[1]

Dr Trevelyan adds, a few sentences later, that 'the abolition of the native upper class to make room for English landlords, begun under the Tudors and completed by Cromwell, left this peasant nation with no leaders but the priests and no sympathisers but the enemies of England'. This gives to Irish Romanism, as we have suggested in an earlier chapter, a unique character. Elsewhere in Europe the popular revolu-tionary movements have tended to be vigorously anticlerical. The rising proletariat has identified the Roman Catholic Church with the forces resisting change. In Ireland that Church has been a Church of the peasant; its priests have been the natural leaders of the proletarian community; its

[1] G. M. Trevelyan, *History of England* (Longmans), p. 362.

faith has been the recognisable common bond of the rebels against English dominance. Such anticlericalism as there has been as, for example, in Sean O'Casey's plays, has been of a latter-day type. It has followed the success of the rebellion. It partakes of the nature of Hyde Park Corner republican oratory. The Roman Catholic Church in Ireland is entrenched in the hearts of its members as it can only be where priests and people have shared a common struggle. There the religious orders of priests have small place. It is the secular, parochial clergy that is in the ascendancy. That clergy has never been recruited from the aristocracy, which was always of an alien faith. It has sprung, like that of the Church of Scotland, from the ranks of the people themselves. In contrast with the Scottish Church there has been small emphasis upon cultural and academic training. The Irish priest has possessed the virtue of dogged faithfulness rather than intellectual power. Thus, for all its rebellious past, Irish Romanism is of an intensely conservative type, little touched by such European novelties as the Liturgical Movement (although there is word, as we write, of a vernacular version of the Mass being published). In the Republic of Ireland the Roman Catholic Church has a position of special recognition which is set forth in the Constitution of 1937.

Until 1871, when it was disestablished by an act of Parliament introduced by Gladstone, the Anglican Church had been the established Church of the island, as part after 1801 of the United Church of England and Ireland. It had never been the Church of more than a minority, and with the growth of tolerance and the revelation by the census of 1861 of the small number of its adherents, it had become intolerable that this status and all the ancient endowments of the Christian Church in Ireland should be possessed by a Church with so small a claim to be in fact the Church of the Irish people.

The act of disestablishment was nevertheless not an easy

one. It is one of the odd anomalies of religious history that the Tractarian movement, so often popularly identified with Romanising tendencies, began with John Keble's sensational Assize sermon on 'National Apostasy'. For the apostasy in question was the action of Parliament in re-ordering some parts of the life of the Church of Ireland, and securing the resources for doing so by the suppression of two archbishoprics (Cashel and Tuam) and the union of a number of dioceses. This reduction in the top-heavy (and, indeed, scandalously over-paid) hierarchy may seem to us an obvious enough step in a country whose inhabitants chiefly belonged to another Church. To Keble and his friends the Roman allegiance of the Irish peasantry was as nothing compared with the sheer sacrilege of the secular arm being laid upon the Ark of God.

Despite this feeling, it was a High Churchman who brought about the disestablishment of the Church of Ireland. Gladstone's biographer, Morley, quotes with approval as delicious an example of Victorian lack of proportion as will readily be found:

> It was true to say that 'never were the wheels of legislative machinery set in motion under conditions of peace and order and constitutional regularity to deal with a question greater or more profound', than when the historic protestant church in Ireland was severed from its sister church in England and from its ancient connection with the state.[1]

This echo of the past, however, reveals the seriousness with which such a step was contemplated and undertaken.

Undoubtedly this sense of seriousness, and the rigid regard which the Victorians had for the rights of property, led to far better terms in regard to disendowment than the Welsh Church was to experience forty years later. Half a million pounds were handed over in lieu of recent endowments, but the big step was the offer of life annuities to all

[1] *Life of Gladstone*, vol. ii, p. 257.

bishops and clergy, who, to their honour be it said, commuted them for the future benefit of the Church. The resultant capital sum, skilfully invested and greatly augmented by the generosity of the laity of the disestablished Church, has certainly enabled the Church of Ireland to maintain a more nation-wide witness than would otherwise have been possible.

As well as the task of material reconstruction, the Church had to face after the Act of 1869 the remaking of the pattern of its life. A convention of bishops, clergy and laity met in the following year to prepare for the coming into force of the act in 1871. It made plain then its basic stand in the pre-amble and declaration which preface the constitution.

> The Church of Ireland doth, as heretofore, accept and unfeignedly believe all the Canonical Scriptures of the Old and New Testament, as given by inspiration of God, and containing all things necessary for salvation; and doth continue to profess the Faith of Christ as professed by the Primitive Church.

It adopted the Thirty-Nine Articles and the Book of Common Prayer, thus firmly linking itself in spirit with the Church of England from which it was to be severed in law. In marked contrast, however, to the larger sister Church it gave the laity an equal part with the clergy in the whole government of the Church, and achieved a uniformity of worship. The Irish Church's version of the Prayer Book, published in 1879, specified the north side of the Holy Table as the place from which the prayer of consecration was to be said, and forbade the placing of a cross on or behind the Holy Table. Anglicanism in a situation of Roman Catholic dominance has naturally always reacted into an emphasis upon its Protestant heritage. It is to the credit of those responsible for guiding the Irish Church's decisions in the time of crisis that this reaction was kept in bounds.

It is the mode of celebration and the absence of the ornaments and vestments which are elsewhere common in an even moderate Anglicanism which have sometimes misled the casual observer about the Church of Ireland. True, the uniformity which the Church of Ireland gained by these provisions was paid for by a certain aridity not normally characteristic of Anglican worship. It must nevertheless not be mistaken for evidence of a 'Low Church' position theologically. It is not always easy to disentangle the High Church theology of the Church of Ireland from its unconscious assumption of continuing privilege. Erastianism on both sides of the Channel can assume a Catholic disguise. But there is in the Church of Ireland a strong High Church tradition. Even before the recovery of that position in England by the Tractarians, Alexander Knox (1757-1831) had been emphasising that the Anglican Church was not a Protestant Church, but a reformed part of the Church Catholic. That conviction is strongly represented in the Church of Ireland today, for all its outward appearance of a very Protestant emphasis.

The ninety years since disestablishment have seen prodigious changes. Many Anglicans left the country during the anarchic years which followed the Easter Rebellion of 1916. Most Protestants have tended since the establishment of the Irish Free State (later to become the Republic of Ireland) to feel that the Six Counties provided more of a spiritual home. The change in the distribution of the Anglican population is vividly illustrated in the following sentence: 'Before Disestablishment in 1871, 54% of our Church members lived in the Twenty-six Counties and 46% in the Six Counties; to-day 70% live in Northern Ireland and only 30% in the Republic of Ireland'.[1] Thus while it was revealed in the census of 1861 that only one-eighth of the population of Ireland then belonged to that Church which was established by law, that eighth was spread throughout the country. Now it has been described as in danger of becoming 'a Church of the

---

[1] W. G. Wilson, *Church Teaching: A Handbook for Members of the Church of Ireland* (APCK), p. 105.

North with a Southern appendix'. Some of the dioceses in the Republic have little more than twenty clergy in them, and the task of ministering to scattered handfuls of Anglicans is made no easier by the atmosphere of decayed past ascendancy which is exactly caught by John Betjeman in the verse at the head of this chapter. The Church of Ireland has about it something of an eighteenth-century flavour. Nowhere will there be found such a plethora of Anglican dignitaries, and nowhere will they be seen more scrupulously arrayed in gaitered glory. Yet, as Bishop Stephen Neill says, 'What strikes the English visitor to Ireland, in his first contact with the Church, is the intensity of the loyalty of both clergy and lay people to their Church.'[1]

Irish Presbyterianism and Methodism

It might be thought that in such a situation—with, in the Republic, the constant setting of Roman Catholic dominance, and in the Six Counties the bogey that the increase in Roman Catholic population will one day tilt the scales—the Anglican, Presbyterian and Methodist Churches would be drawn very readily together in co-operation and even union. But this is to reckon without Irish church history, and a tangle of sociological and historical factors in Christian disunity of daunting complexity. This is especially visible in Anglican-Presbyterian relations. The two Churches are of approximately equal size. Presbyterianism in Ireland dates from the opening of the seventeenth century and the Plantation of Ulster. It was therefore in Antrim and Down that the Calvinist faith became established, and Presbyterianism was for long dominantly a Church of rural communities. The tragic history of the religious struggle throughout that century in England and Scotland was repeated in Ireland, including an eviction of Presbyterian ministers at the Restoration. A happier chapter began with the grant by Charles II of £600

[1] *Anglicanism*, p. 297.

a year to be shared amongst the Presbyterian ministers, which naturally a grateful King William after the flight of James II doubled. This royal patronage did not, however, bring legal toleration; and it is almost incredible that in face of the Roman Catholic hold on the country the Anglican established Church should have clung so tenaciously to an indefensible position. (There is a particularly unhappy chapter about the recognition of Presbyterian marriages.)

Presbyterianism, however, was also weakened from within by controversy over subscription to the Confessions, and by the development of those divisions, reproduced from Scotland, which gave it for so long a fissiparous character.

Presbyterianism in Ireland was for long in two minds. Although ecclesiastically and theologically at the other extreme from Roman Catholicism, its members shared much of the experience of the members of that Church. Professor J. M. Barkley writes:

> In the second half of the eighteenth century the Romanists, under the Penal Code, were treated as aliens in their native land, and they had no political rights; and the Presbyterians were excluded from all civil, military, and municipal offices by the Test Act, except indemnified.[1]

In such a situation it was inevitable that Presbyterians and Romanists should sometimes make common cause against the privileged Establishment.

On the other hand the development during the succeeding century of the demand for Irish Home Rule tended to bring second thoughts to Presbyterians. 'Home Rule', in the current phrase, would be 'Rome Rule'. So, although the Orange Society, or Order, came into being in 1795 chiefly on the initiative of Anglicans, as the nineteenth century wore on and the civil disabilities of Presbyterians were relieved and at the same time the prospect for Home Rule under the

---

[1] *A Short History of the Presbyterian Church in Ireland* (Presbyterian Church in Ireland), p. 34.

ascendancy of Gladstone became bright, the Order attracted Presbyterians in large numbers. By the last quarter of the century, in any case, the privileges of the Church of Ireland were no more.

Nevertheless the past history of ejectment and civil disability remained to stultify good relations on the Presbyterian side, while the knowledge that Presbyterians had united from time to time with Romanists against their fellow Protestants rankled in Episcopalian breasts. And the native air of Ireland has ever been excellent for the preservation of the memory.

One strange result of the disestablishment of the Church of Ireland on Presbyterian fortunes was to make its state endowment the most lavish of all Churches in Britain that have not been established. The annual royal gift, the *Regium Donum,* was commuted for a lump sum, amounting to well over £500,000, and generous provision was also made by the Government for the theological education of Presbyterian ministers. (Similar provision was made for the Roman Catholic Church.)

The Presbyterian Church in Ireland, which took the form in which we know it today by the union of two bodies in 1840, holds the doctrine and possesses the government of all Presbyterian Churches which owe their origin to Scotland. It has, however, a character all its own in a number of ways. It was immensely affected by what is called the Ulster Revival of 1859. The previous year a great wave of revival swept over part of North America. Many of Ulster's sons, like many from other parts of Ireland, had sought their fortune in the New World; so it was natural that the movement should spread by letters home speaking of spiritual experience. The sober judgment of Principal J. E. Davey, writing in 1940, is:

> The great bulk of the Christian workers of the Irish Presbyterian Church for the next generation came from those who had been touched by the movement. The work of 1859 and the years which followed gave a new life to the religion of Ulster, a new enthu-

siasm and a new power—its influence was not evanescent as the influence of such movements unfortunately sometimes is.[1]

The Revival, which was marked by disturbing prenomena of a psychological sort, had its most positive result in an Evangelical warmth being given to Irish Presbyterianism, such as Calvinist religion has not always possessed. On the other hand, Principal Davey does not deny some truth in the suggestion 'that the evangelistic temper promoted by the Revival has predisposed many to obscurantism, to a contempt for education and an unscientific credulity of mind not far removed from that of Romanism, and an over-emphasis on excitement and on attempts to produce it artificially'. That does not mean that the artificial production of excitement is found in Presbyterianism, but certainly some of the appeal of the revivalist gospel halls so commonly found in Northern Ireland can be attributed to the yearning for emotionalism.

Presbyterianism in Ireland—like other Churches there—sometimes reveals a concern with questions of personal behaviour of a kind which used to be found in Victorian England. Such issues as whether ministers of religion should be seen smoking on the television screen, or the propriety of clerical attendance at the theatre, will engage serious attention. This is symptomatic not only of the strength of the Puritan tradition in Irish Protestantism, but even more of the secure place that religion still has in the community. Peripheral questions of this type are only of interest to those who have not yet been exposed to the full blast of secularism. Such is still the position in Ireland. The working man can still be found in the churches of Ulster. The minister is still a man who commands instant respect, whose figure, clothed on any occasion of important clerical duty in the frock coat only seen in England at royal garden parties, represents the continuing strength of the place of religion in the country.

Great changes nonetheless are coming over Irish Pres-

[1] *1840-1940: The Story of a Hundred Years,* pp. 41-2.

byterianism. Of the three main Protestant Churches it has always been, by reason of the plantation of Antrim and Down, a dominantly Ulster Church. It has possessed little strength outside the North, save for a few vigorous congregations in Dublin. This has been rendered even more true by the political change of this century. Presbyterians have been closely identified with the political cause of Ulster. More than one Presbyterian minister has, in fact, held cabinet office in the government of Northern Ireland. It has become customary for religious observances by that Government to be equally shared between the Church of Ireland and the Presbyterian Church, which have come, by reason of their roughly equal strength, to have some informal national recognition.

But an even bigger change has been from a rural to an urban Church. Now some half of the whole population of the Six Counties is within the environs of Belfast, and indeed the strength of the Presbyterian Church, which was for obvious historical reasons to be found in the rural communities of the settled areas, is now chiefly to be found in that one industrial city.

Irish Methodism, while sharing the non-episcopal tradition of Presbyterianism, was markedly different in history and geographical distribution. It arises not from any Protestant settlement or plantation but, like English Methodism, from the direct work of the Wesleys. John Wesley from 1747 onwards made twenty-one journeys to Ireland. His stay there was often for a considerable period. Even before the founder's visit, some of his followers had been engaged in work in Dublin and beyond. It is to be noted that Irish Methodism did not begin in the North. The first chapel opened was in Dublin. The first Irish Methodist Conference was held under the presidency of John Wesley in 1752. He often exercised that office in later years, and even today, although there is a President of the Methodist Church in Ireland, it is the President of the British Conference who chiefly presides over the Irish body. Despite this close link, Irish Methodism has developed its own separate life, and there has been very little interchange of ministers across the Irish Sea. Because of the close affinity of Methodist origins with the Anglican Church, the spread of Methodism has tended to be more nation-wide than Presbyterianism, although numbers have always been small. The circuit system and the use of local preachers assisted this geographical spread by enabling quite small communities to be maintained. The potato famine in the middle of the last century sadly reduced Irish Methodism in numbers. To-day the Methodist Church has only 30,000 members, but Methodism has played a far larger part in the religious life of Ireland than that would suggest. Like the other Protestant Churches it has tended to diminish rapidly in the Republic and to grow in numbers in the north-eastern corner.[1]

No part of our islands has shown the kind of change that Ireland has done. That change during the last century was indeed diametrically opposed to that of Britain. In Britain during the nineteenth century, as we earlier remarked, the population quadrupled. During the same period in Ireland it was halved. This century has seen political change that has divided the island into two, and made the southern half a republic. It can scarcely be wondered at that the state of the Churches there today bears little relation to what is found in the other island. It is sad that the situation which, most urgently in the Republic, has demanded the consolidation of all Protestant forces has too little evoked a spirit of active unity. The memories of the past remain too strong to permit the response which the needs of tiny Protestant communities in southern Ireland demand. But there have been recent

[1] The percentage of its increase in Northern Ireland is larger because of its earlier distribution. The 1951 census revealed that there had been the following increases during 1937-51: Church of Ireland, 2.2%; Roman Catholic Church, 10%; Presbyterian, 4.9%; Methodist, 20.7%. See W. G. Wilson, *op. cit.*, p. 108.

moves between Presbyterians and Methodists which may prove harbingers of a happier day. Both in the new housing areas around Belfast and in the scattered rural communities of the Republic joint work is being undertaken by these two Churches. And there are signs that the common experience of the ecumenical movement is moving some leaders of both episcopal and non-episcopal Churches to closer fellowship. It remains true that the more traditionally religious condition of Ireland has preserved a vehemence in holding theological positions which has been diminished in Churches which have been more exposed to the chilling wind of secularism. That grim experience may come to the Irish Churches before long.

6

THE CHURCHES IN WALES

'In a large and comfortable kitchen I found a middle-aged woman seated by a huge deal table near a blazing fire, with a couple of large books open before her. Sitting down upon a chair I told her in English to bring me a pint of ale. She did so, and again sat down to her books, which on enquiry I found to be a Welsh Bible and Concordance.'

George Borrow, Wild Wales.

The Welsh Religious Awakening

The English holiday-maker in Wales has all the pleasure of foreign travel at small expense. In most parts of the country he hears a strange language being spoken in the streets and the shops, and it is this language which adorns the mysterious notice boards of the innumerable chapels. If he finds himself in rural Wales on a Sunday he will quickly be made aware that Sabbatarianism is no outmoded shibboleth there. Dark Sunday clothes and a sober decorum mark those who make their way to the stark buildings bearing such biblical names as Carmel and Bethel, from which comes the sound of hymn-singing of a fervour and beauty rarely to be heard from English sanctuaries.

The Englishman in fact is conscious of being religiously as well as linguistically in a strange land. Once again the sharp contrasts which are evident between the four countries which make up the British Isles appear. In Ireland the Reformation never became a nationally accepted movement. In Scotland the events of the sixteenth century imparted an indelible character to both Church and nation. In Wales it was the eighteenth century which determined the character of Welsh culture and religion. The mountainous character of the country and the fact that her peasantry spoke another language than English made Wales less accessible to change. Towards the close of Elizabeth's reign the eventual instruments of the great eighteenth-century movement were provided. They were the Bible and the Book of Common Prayer in the Welsh tongue. But a century and a half were to pass before they made their full impact.

'In the Eighteenth Century the Welsh people recovered, through the instrumentality of religion and education, the consciousness of a spiritual and intellectual life of their own, separate from that of England.'[1] It is important to note the strong connection between religion and education. It was not just that the Churches were the first means of popular education, as in England. A closer parallel is to be found in the development of education on the mission fields of Asia and Africa in the nineteenth century, where it was recognised that a strong and vital religion had to be nourished by Bible reading, which implied a literate Church. A particular phenomenon in Wales was the circulating school, founded by Griffith Jones (1683-1761), rector of Llanddowror, the basis of which was the travelling teacher whose work was to instruct both adults and children so that they could read the Welsh Bible. By the time he died over 3,000 of these schools were in existence. They were a tremendous force in the whole religious awakening of Wales.

That awakening was part of the spiritual quickening which we call the Methodist revival, but it had its own Welsh leader, and it appears that his conversion was not directly related to the work of the Oxford Methodists. That leader was Howel Harris, and his conversion was in 1735. His diary makes no mention of the Oxford Methodists until October, 1737, and it was not until eighteen months after that that he met George Whitefield, the leader of the Calvinist development

[1] G. M. Trevelyan, *English Social History*, p. 368.

of the revival, in contrast with the Arminian doctrine which characterised the work of the Wesleys themselves. So the revival in Wales can reasonably be described as a spontaneous movement, although one which before long became related to the larger one afoot in England. Even then it was linked to the side of it which came to have less influence in England. Although Whitefield was incomparably the greater orator, he did not compare with John Wesley in that genius for organization which has made Methodism the strong body that it is. Associated with Whitefield was that dominating 'Elect Lady', Selina, Countess of Huntingdon, who has the unique distinction for a woman of having given her name to an English denomination, the Countess of Huntingdon's Connexion, which survives today in very attentuated form.

In the later part of Howel Harris' life the Countess of Huntingdon gave her strong support to his work. It is in Wales that Calvinistic Methodism became a great force, and the revival that brought it into being greatly stirred and vitalised the older Dissent, both Independent and Baptist.[1]

With Howel Harris were associated Griffith Jones, of the circulating schools (who paid for his Methodism by having his licence suspended by the Bishop of St Davids) and Daniel Rowlands. Although the first Association in 1743 was held before John Wesley's first conference, the disinclination of these Calvinistic Methodists to part company with the Anglican Church was if anything more marked than that of their Arminian brethren in England. Not until 1811 was the final step of separation taken by the ordination of ministers. This was indeed a movement of renewal within the Church. Only when persecution drove them to take the reluctant step of registering their meeting places as Dissenting chapels,

[1] The older Nonconformist Churches in Wales are of considerable strength. The Baptist Churches in Wales possess some 75,000 members; the Union of Welsh Independents, towards 125,000. (The Presbyterian Church of Wales—Calvinistic Methodist—has about 150,000 members.)

to gain the protection of the law, and insufficient sympathetic priests were to be found to minister to them the sacraments, did the parting of the ways come. The earlier literature of the movement gives ample evidence of the determination, which only circumstances broke down, not to be associated with Dissent, but with the Church itself.

The direct result of this movement therefore was not that renewal of the Anglican Church itself which was purposed, but the creation of a new Church which came to play an immense part in the development of modern Wales. The Calvinistic Methodist, or Presbyterian, Church of Wales is an interesting body ecclesiastically. It is the one Presbyterian Church in these islands which owes its origin not directly to the Calvinist side of the Reformation but to the Methodist revival in its Calvinist aspect. It can even be reasonably claimed that it is the one Presbyterian Church in the Commonwealth which does not owe its origin to Scottish Presbyterianism. Although Presbyterian in government, and possessing a confession of faith directly related to the Westminster Confession, its bears many marks of its origin in a movement of revival rather than of ecclesiastical reform. Revival has marked the continuing story of the Church, as it has of those older Dissenting bodies with which the Calvinistic Methodists came increasingly to have many links and common purposes. The most recent of those recurrent movements was in 1904, which began with the transforming religious experience of Evan Roberts in a Calvinistic Methodist chapel near Aber-porth. The resultant movement swept through Wales like a forest fire.

With a heritage like that it is not surprising that the Presbyterian Church of Wales sits more lightly to the structures of denominational life than the other Presbyterian Churches. The General Assembly is indeed only a deliberative and not a legislative body. Power resides in the quarterly Associations. For long there were two—for the North and the South. (It must be remembered that Wales is greatly divided by its central mountain *massif*. Meetings between North and South Wales commonly take place in Shrewsbury!) In recent years a third Association, of the East, has been added. This is only roughly geographical in basis, and comprises the considerable number of English-speaking congregations, many of which are in England itself.

Anglicanism in Wales

Even after the translation of the Prayer Book and the Bible into Welsh, the Anglican Church has had an unhappy history in the Principality. We call a bishop to bear witness:

> English treatment of Wales was generally scurvy. Many bishops appointed to Welsh sees were non-resident. A Welsh bishopric was often regarded as no more than a steppingstone on the way to a better bishopric in England. Translations were unreasonably frequent. Even among the best and most devoted bishops, many could not speak Welsh, and were therefore cut off from intimate ministration to their flocks; for in Wales the Welsh language has remained a living instrument ... In consequence of all this the Church lost ground, and the non-Anglican bodies, notably the Calvinistic Methodists, gained where the Church had lost. The Church had become no more than a privileged minority.[1]

The fact that the great eighteenth-century renewal of Welsh culture and religion was founded upon the use of the Welsh language meant that it flowed into the channels of those Churches and religious societies which commonly used it, and were identified with Wales, and did not bear the appearance of an English institution. The immense growth of Welsh Nonconformity, and the fact that it expressed both the national feelings and the religious experience of the great majority of the Welsh people, was bound to lead to the privileged position of the Anglican establishment being rudely challenged. Challenged it was, and in the van of the protagonists of Welsh disestablishment was David Lloyd George.

[1] Stephen Neill, *Anglicanism*, p. 317.

His experiences as a solicitor in fighting tithe-exactments supplied munitions for the fight. His power as a leading minister in the Liberal Governments from 1906 onwards sounded the doom of the establishment in Wales. In any case 31 out of the 34 Welsh M.P.s returned in the two elections after 1909 were pledged to seek disestablishment. The deed was done in 1914 although, on account of the War, the act did not become operative until six years later. Then the Church in Wales as it is today came into being, a separate province of the Anglican communion (previously it had been part of the province of Canterbury).

There can be no doubt that disestablishment has been for the spiritual good of Wales. Bitterness was inevitable against the establishment of a minority Church possessed of great privileges, and able to exact tithes from those whose allegiance lay elsewhere (and whose own churches had to be supported by their voluntary giving). The past forty years have seen the great diminution of that, and some recognition at least of the contribution that Anglican worship can make to Welsh religion. Certainly the challenge of disestablishment has revitalised the Church in Wales itself. (It is by the title, perhaps a little presumptuous, of 'the Church in Wales' that the new province of the Anglican Communion in Wales chose to be called.)

There were originally four dioceses, Bangor, Llandaff, St Asaph and St Davids. Two more were added at the time of disestablishment—Monmouth, and Swansea and Brecon. There is an Archbishop of Wales, chosen from amongst the diocesan bishops. The laity—men and women—are fully joined with the episcopate and the clergy in the government of the Church, and the generosity both of money and of talent which the laity has displayed in the disestablished Church has been notable. Considerable disendowment accompanied disestablishment, and there has been a great struggle to maintain the Church's structure with decreased resources. A considerable drain upon the Church's finance has been the training of clergy who eventually seek to minister in the Church of England, where circumstances tend to be a good deal easier. Not a few of the present-day clergy, and even some of the recent bishops, have originated from Nonconformity. They have been able to discern a truly Welsh Church in the contemporary Church in Wales as perhaps the previous generation could scarcely have done.

The Church in Wales tends to be both 'high' and a little self-conscious. Both traits are readily understandable. The dominance in the whole religious scene of Nonconformity creates an inevitable reaction, and the newness of the Church in its present form and its commendable determination to be fully identified with Welsh life and language lead to a certain self-consciousness in its claims and attitudes. Possibly its greatest contributions to the religious life of Wales could be in the realm of worship and unity. The culture which the chapels have nourished has been a culture of the ear rather than the eye. In poetry, hymn and song they have made a great contribution to the recovery and reinstatement of a genuine Welsh culture. They have suffered from the typical Calvinist suspicion of that beauty which must be apprehended through the eyes. The Welsh chapel is not a thing of loveliness. Here the Church in Wales has a complementary word to say.

In regard to unity, we can well imagine that many Welsh Free Churchmen would smile at the idea that the Church in Wales has a particular message, for it is generally regarded as obdurate in the extreme. Nevertheless it has the characteristic Anglican challenge to offer, even if sometimes it is given unnecessarily unpalatably. It stands for a belief in the organic unity of the Church in a land where the other Churches have settled down to a regrettable acceptance of division. The average Welsh village of any size is dotted with a diversity of chapels. The old theological reasons for division between Baptist, Independent, and Calvinistic Methodist no longer grip men's minds, but there are all too few signs of any resolute tackling of the wasteful and harmful divisions of Welsh religious life.

The Free Churches Today

It is difficult to find a suitable word to describe the non-episcopal Welsh Churches today. 'Nonconformist' has historic meaning, but used today implies an establishment which is no longer there. So indeed does the word 'Free Churches', but at least it seems acceptable to the Churches themselves, which are members of the Free Church Federal Council of England and Wales. It is certainly those Churches which have made Wales what it is today, whatever larger part may be played in the future by the Church in Wales in its new form.

The link between revival and education in the eighteenth century has meant that the characteristic Free Church family sets a high value upon education. That has had one striking effect in the mining valleys and other parts of industrialised Wales where the chapels were often for long the only places of worship. It is often said that the miners built the chapels and then left them. It would be interesting to discover how general is the experience which one Welsh Free Church minister recently revealed to us from an examination of the occupations of his church members in the last generation and this. (It was in a relatively static community.) In the last generation the members and office-bearers had chiefly been men who worked with their hands. Today they were chiefly professional and white-collar workers. *But many of them were the sons of the former members.* Miners who had shared in the popular culture that centred in the chapel swore that their sons should have greater opportunities than they had had, and made great sacrifices to that end.

Certainly one effect of this has been that while the Nonconformist chapels were the heart of the Liberal political

party, and nourished many of the Welsh pioneers of social-
ism, they have failed to hold the working-class movement as
a whole. They have tended to create a division not of class but
of seriousness. The serious group 'includes the roadman or
farm labourer who is a Sunday School teacher and deacon,
and whose children are given the best education that circumstances allow—often better than they allow'.[1] This is possible
in a rural community, but the solidarity of union-organised
labour in the great industries has probably worked against
any such division in urban areas.

Seriousness marked the chapel-goer in many ways. He
was strictly a total abstainer and an observer of the Sabbath.
Yet nothing could be more untrue than to think of the
chapel-goers as living an impoverished and restricted life.
Although the new member would be described as received
o'r byd, i.e. from 'the world', and there was a strong Puritan
emphasis, around the chapel grew the community's cultural
life and entertainment. The great gift of Wales to the world
in singing, and above all her glorious and haunting hymns,
was nourished in the rough chapels of the Nonconformist
Churches.

Even today in rural Wales the chapel, if not as central in
people's lives as it once was, retains a power to mould society
that is unknown in any religious body in England. In the
towns and cities the corrosions of modern life have been
more evidently at work, and the problem of the Churches
there is probably chiefly that of disentangling themselves from
the irrelevant parts of the heritage of past dominance. There
is much evidence of doubts and questioning in the Welsh Free
Churches today. A ministry to which the accepted results of
a reasonable biblical criticism are part of normal thought
sometimes feels hindered by a body of deacons whose faith
is founded upon a fundamentalist view of scripture. These

[1] David Jenkins in *Welsh Rural Communities,* ed. E. Davies and
A. D. Rees (University of Wales Press), p. 17.

churches have given a great place to the elder or deacon, visibly symbolised by their special place in the chapel, near the pulpit—the 'big pew'. It has been a considerable strength in the past. There are those today who doubt whether the balance between ministerial and lay responsibility has been rightly struck.

There are parts of Wales too, where the language question is a problem. For example, in Glamorgan there are chapels which are reluctant to change to the use of English, although it is now the natural language of the younger generation, because the older generation who are the support of the chapel have their religious and devotional life rooted in Welsh. There would even be many among the younger ministers who would strive hard against the loss of Welsh, seeing in it one further step away from the retention of a culture in which the Welsh spirit can truly be nourished towards an Anglicising that would destroy the peculiar Welsh contribution to the Christian Church.

Altogether the Welsh Churches face a period when the securities which a few decades ago seemed so strong are being rudely challenged. A land wherein a genuine popular culture has been developed within its own indigenous forms of religious life is bound to be one which suffers more acutely the insidious invasions of the secularisation and mass-culture of this century. It is hard to believe that renewal can come to the Welsh Churches without some resolute facing of the present divisions. Most of all, the question abides whether the Welsh Churches can begin to play a larger part in the wider counsels of the Churches of Britain and beyond, and still preserve their own riches.

7

'EVANGELICALS ALL'

'As I walked through the wilderness of this world, I lighted on a certain place where was a Den, and I laid me down in that place to sleep: and, as I slept, I dreamed a dream. I dreamed, and behold, I saw a man clothed with rags, standing in a certain place, with his face from his own house, a book in his hand, and a great burden upon his back ... and, not being able longer to contain, he brake out with a lamentable cry, saying, *What shall I do?'*   *John Bunyan,* The Pilgrim's Progress.

Conservative Evangelicals

THIS opening passage of the greatest of all English religious allegories represents a historic and continuing strand in the Christian life of these islands. Naturally enough, in a book of this title, we have been concerned in the preceding pages with British Christian experience in its ecclesiastical, institutional aspect. It has been our purpose to display, as adequately as our compass allows, British churchmanship in its history, variety and inter-relationship. But the great strand of intense, individual Evangelical experience defies the categories we have used hitherto. It is both within many of the Churches in the 'main stream' of the Christian tradition which we have been describing, and beyond them. Wherever it is found it is characterised by a marked disregard for the institutional side of religion, and a great stress upon the saving word of the Gospel. Above all, the great emphasis is upon the costly redemption won for sinners by Christ upon his cross. It is a strand that is intertwined with our national religious life from Wyclif and his Poor Preachers in the fourteenth century, to Dr Billy Graham in London's Harringay Arena or Glasgow's Kelvin Hall.

These 'evangelicals all' are in every age men with a Book in their hands. From Wyclif pleading for the Bible to be translated into English, to Dr Graham saying 'The Bible says . . .,' this is a constant element. Today this means that most Evangelicals are in varying degrees suspicious of modern biblical criticism. The very word suggests to them an overweening human pride that fails to recognise that 'the fear of the Lord, that is wisdom'. Certainly there have been excessive scepticisms in the past in biblical study which have given some colour to the suggestion. The word 'fundamentalist' is often used to describe this school of Evangelicals, but it is a clumsy, and often pejorative, word. 'Conservative Evangelicals' is another phrase. Neither serves well, but the latter suggests something of their position. For them the authority of the Bible is final, and, while they vary a good deal among themselves in the degree of literalism which they attach to scriptural inspiration, they are all agreed that the old way of reading the Bible is the best. Their understanding of Evangelical truth is also a particular one. Certain marks are to be seen in the true Christian as they recognise him. Central beliefs are a doctrine of the atonement which emphasises that God accepted Christ's substitution of himself for wrath-deserving sinners in receiving the punishment of the cross, and the physical second coming of the Lord. Separation from 'the world', chiefly in abstention from such activities as dancing, the consumption of alcohol, most entertainments and smoking, is seen as the natural result of being 'twice-born'.

The glory of this school of thought has been seen in a degree of Christian commitment which sometimes out-classes that of other Christians. Often such Evangelicals are prepared to offer themselves in sacrificial Christian service in impressive numbers. That redemption of men and society which can be achieved by consecrated individuals has received a great contribution from them. Where such Evangelicals have made little impact is in that penetration of the culture and activities of society which calls for both deeper engagement with the world, and a closer study of its problems that the simple formulas of the Conservative Evangelical admit. British Christianity would be greatly the poorer if their emphasis had been lacking. It is to be regretted that many, though certainly not all, have been exclusive in their attitudes, and therefore have denied to the larger body of Christians their challenge and enrichment.

One organisation which has powerfully reinforced this strand of Christian belief is the Inter-Varsity Fellowship, with its branches, usually known as Christian Unions, in most universities. It is the IVF which has produced many of the leaders of the movement. It has stood for a great deal in the past, and is a very flourishing organisation in the universities today. The very positiveness of the dogmatic approach of the Fellowship commends it to young men and women seeking religious truth which is not relative, but authoritative and final. It has a fine record in evoking vocations to missionary service oversea. It is less pleasing that it has proved often unwilling to combine in any common activity, including even joint intercession, with Christians within the universities of different allegiance and approach.

Although the IVF and similar Conservative Evangelical groupings can rightly be described as inter-denominational, they are not ecumenical, and indeed are on the whole rather unhappy about, if not opposed to, the modern ecumenical movement. That movement is based upon the conviction that churchmanship matters, and that the loyalty we have to our own Church must be taken with great seriousness. On the basis of a common commitment to Christ, even before there is any defined doctrinal agreement, we are called together to seek a visible unity. That search must be on the basis of an honest recognition of ecclesiastical differences and the treasure in differing church traditions.

The Conservative Evangelical groupings tend to deny this at several points. They do not believe that true fellowship is possible save on the basis of a thorough agreement on Evangelical doctrines such as we have enunciated as their particular marks. Given that agreement, they do not believe that differences of church tradition signify. As Stephen Neill has said of the great Evangelical movements of the nineteenth century:

> Another approach . . . was to say that denominations really do not matter very much; the all-important thing is faith in Christ, and, if we are agreed on that, we need not talk very much about the details of those things which divide us. In the task of witnessing to Christ we find ourselves completely at one.[1]

In fact the Conservative Evangelicals—or certainly the exclusive element among them—represent a horizontal division between Christians. There are the vertical divisions between separate denominations. This other is a division which cuts across the denominations. The achievement of Christian unity would not be complete if all the separate Churches were miraculously to become one, unless the gulf that often exists between the Conservative Evangelicals and others remained unbridged.

There is a very considerable part of the Church of England which falls within this description. We have ourselves had experience of the Evangelical congregation of a parish church which had much more real fellowship with the local Brethren hall and Baptist church than with the neighbouring 'high' parish of its own Communion. It is commonly said by Anglicans that the campaigns in London of Dr Graham drew their support chiefly from Nonconformist sources. This is more than doubtful. There seems a good deal of evidence that the Evangelical Anglican parishes supplied very great support. The absence of any theological colleges in most of the Free Churches which impart this particular teaching has

[1] *Men of Unity* (SCM Press), p. 18.

lessened its hold upon them. Although there are certainly plenty of Conservative Evangelicals in Baptist and Methodist churches, it is far from being a specifically Free Church position.

In addition to those who hold these views within the Churches of the 'main stream', there are smaller Churches and Christian bodies which are, as it were, corporate expressions of these convictions. In the remainder of this short chapter we turn to three of them.

The Salvation Army

One such body makes a strong public impact. It is the Salvation Army, which historically is one of the radical off-shoots of nineteenth-century Methodism. Under God, it was the result of the work of yet another of those original religious geniuses of which our pragmatic race has been so strangely productive, William Booth (1829-1912). After being a local preacher with the Wesleyan Methodists he became a minister of the Methodist New Connexion, the first of the separations from the original body of Methodist people. It never became large, but has the distinction of having nurtured the founder of the most unconventional of world-wide religious movements. Booth's concern was with those in our great and fantastically growing cities who were living lives submerged in desperate poverty and vice, and who were being touched by neither the established Church nor any of the bodies which did not conform to it. They were a large section of the population. A drastic situation demanded a drastic new strategy, with drastic new techniques. From his earlier experiments grew the Salvation Army. It is one of the most honoured religious bodies of the world today, but the vileness of the organised persecution which the earlier Salvationists endured was the measure of the effectiveness of their challenge to the vicious influences in society.

It was in 1878 that the name was first adopted and the

mission recognised as being 'to carry the Blood of Christ and the Fire of the Holy Ghost to every corner of the world'. The 'Blood and Fire' banner now floats in the breezes of towards a hundred countries, and the army now has some 17,000 corps and outposts throughout the world.

At the heart of the Army lie two convictions. One is of the saving power of orthodox Evangelical Christian doctrine; the other is that any honourable method is justified that will break through to those who are unaffected by the message as proclaimed by the Churches. Thus the Army is indeed an army, organised not only with military titles but with military discipline. Its ordinary members are soldiers who are expected to fight the Lord's battles, and not to wait for the full-time officers to do it for them. The officers, usually drawn from that section of society which the Army has evangelised, are trained for the conflict and hold themselves ready to be moved almost without notice from one battle station to another as orders are given by their superiors. The Army thus has a power of mobility which, say, the parson's freehold in the Church of England prevents.

One striking innovation of William Booth was his use of women in entire equality with men. This was further evidence of his entire freedom from convention, which went along with an absolute dogmatic conservatism. When it is remembered that the first wearers of the Salvation Army lass's bonnet had to venture into places where no decent girl would normally be seen, and to face the abuse of hired louts, his courage in this innovation will be recognised. He was in many respects the Protestant Ignatius Loyola. Once again, the tragedy is that his work had to be done outside the Church. (It was paid the sincerest form of flattery in 1882 by an Anglican priest, Wilson Carlile, who in that year founded the Church Army on similar lines as an auxiliary of the Church of England.)

An additional aspect of Booth's paradoxical combination of fearless innovation with religious conservatism was his thorough development of social work. Often 'soul salvation' is contrasted by Evangelicals with 'social salvation'. Booth's identification with the 'Darkest England' of which he wrote in a dramatically influential book of that title in 1890 left him with no illusion that it was sufficient to 'preach the Gospel'. Along with the brass bands and the vigorous hymns set to popular airs ('Why should the Devil have all the best tunes?' cried Booth), along with the street corner preaching and the strongly emotional pleas within the Army's citadels to come forward to make a new beginning at the penitent's bench, went homes for prostitutes, food depots and shelters, rescue homes and expert efforts at the reclamation of drunkards and recidivist prisoners. This remarkable social work has been developed and continued to the present day, and constitutes one of the finest expressions of Christian care for those for whom our Lord had a particular tenderness.

The Salvation Army rejects the use of the sacraments. This contrasts it sharply with other Evangelical groupings, such as the Brethren who gather each Lord's Day for the Breaking of Bread. It links the Army somewhat curiously with the Society of Friends, which is in every other way utterly different from the Army (save perhaps in great social concern). It seems a far cry from the Quaker love of silence and unobtrusive ways, to the popular and bold methods of the Army in its determination to win souls. William Booth was baptised an Anglican, and was nurtured, as we have seen, among Methodists. He was not opposed to sacramental religion, but the example of the Society of Friends made him believe that holiness was possible without sacraments, which he saw being made the occasion of division rather than unity between the various Churches. An interesting factor in his decision was the desire to have utter equality of men and women in the Army, and at that time it seemed unthinkable to many that a woman should administer the sacraments. The sacraments had a place in the early days of the movement, but 'the Founder decided that, seeing the sacraments are but symbols of spiritual truth and experience, Salvationists in their own form of worship would not in seeking the substance place emphasis upon the shadow'.[1]

The place of the Army today is an honoured and accepted one in British Church life. Members of the Churches, and indeed men of goodwill outside them, give generously to the Army's work, for it is recognised that Salvationists tackle expertly many jobs which should be done by Christians, and are not effectively done by the ordinary church fellowship. The big question mark over the future is how the Army can adapt its work in Britain to a social situation utterly different from that in which it was first conceived. Can it be used as an effective Christian weapon in a day when vice and social irresponsibility are not the fruits of poverty but flourish within security and affluence? We may admire the gallant traditional witness with band and testimony on the street corner, yet wonder whether it is entirely relevant in the day of the ubiquitous television screen, and whether the Salvation Army may not have to face as drastic changes in its methods as are demanded of the Churches themselves.

The Brethren

As we turn from the Salvation Army to the Brethren, while we remain within the same main theological area—a 'fundamentalist' conviction about the Bible and a thorough-going Puritanism in matters of personal behaviour—in many other ways we enter a wholly different world. They originate in a movement around 1830 in Dublin, in which a central figure was John Nelson Darby, a former priest of the (Anglican) Church of Ireland. One of the first and strongest congregations in England was at Plymouth, and this gave rise to the

[1] *The Sacraments: The Salvationist's Viewpoint* (Salvationist Publishing and Supplies Ltd), pp. 6-7.

popular description under which they are commonly known, 'Plymouth' Brethren. Unlike the Quakers, however, the Brethren themselves have proved unwilling to adopt their nick-name.

One point of contrast with the Army has already been mentioned. The Breaking of Bread is the main act of worship of the Brethren in their gospel halls or rooms each Sunday. Another contrast is in the status of women, who share but little in the work of the body, for the words of Paul in this regard are seen as determinative. The Brethren are allied with the Baptists in practising the baptism of believers only.[1] Most characteristic of the Brethren is a great seriousness and sobriety of mien and conduct.

There is a great division, which occurred in 1849, between 'open' and 'exclusive' or 'closed' Brethren. The latter look with disfavour on the degree to which the former are prepared to co-operate with other Christian bodies. Although even the 'open' Brethren are not to be found within the national or international organs of the ecumenical movement (as, interestingly enough, the Salvation Army is) they certainly gladly associate with other Evangelical groups, and are occasionally to be found in local Councils of Churches. The entire independence of the local congregation and the absence of any organ for drawing them together would in any case militate against membership of wider councils.

The Pentecostal Churches

There remains one other quite considerable grouping of those Evangelicals who are outside the main stream of

---

[1] Those acquainted with that minor classic, Edmund Gosse's *Father and Son,* will recall a picture of the life of the Brethren, to which Gosse *père* belonged, in the Victorian era, and the precocious horror with which the young Gosse exclaims of the pious Anglican lady who is to be his step-mother, 'But, Father, is she a paedo-baptist?'

Churches which earlier chapters have described.[1] These are the Churches usually described under the generic heading 'Pentecostalist'. Their particular importance derives not so much from their numbers (although they are having a notable success in certain parts of our cities in which the other Churches experience frustration), as from their representation of an element in Christian experience which has been increasingly overlooked. Bishop Lesslie Newbigin has questioned whether the usual Catholic-Protestant division is adequate in analysis (and therefore in eventual reconciliation). He adduces a third strand—the Pentecostal.[2] It is natural enough that this reminder should come from an outstanding missionary leader, for the Pentecostal movement has been marked by an immense outpouring of oversea missionary service.

The movement began, unlike those elsewhere described in these pages, without any outstanding leader. It originated in the USA in the early years of this century. In Britain it dates from 1907, and it consists today of two main groupings. They are the Elim Foursquare Gospel Alliance, formed in 1915, and the Assemblies of God in Great Britain and Ireland, formed in 1924. They might be described respectively as the connexional and congregational forms of Pentecostalism, which today in Britain numbers more than 50,000 members, and is a considerable world-wide movement.

The British historian of the movement, Mr Donald Gee, states the scriptural basis as follows:

> The designation 'Pentecostal' arises from its emphasis upon a baptism in the Holy Spirit such as that recorded in Acts 2, that occurred on the Day of Pentecost. The Pentecostal movement shares ... the conviction that such a baptism in the Holy Spirit

[1] Our concern is, of course, with orthodox Evangelicals. Those who have departed from orthodoxy will be found described in *Christian Deviations* by Horton Davies (SCM Press).

[2] *The Household of God* (SCM Press), pp. 87-110.

remains as a separate individual experience possible for all Christians, irrespective of time or place (Acts 2, 38, 39) ... The particular and distinctive testimony of the Pentecostal Movement has been that the outward evidences that accompanied the baptism in the Holy Spirit in primitive Christian experience can be, should be, and are being repeated up to date. It is this special witness that has earned for it among its opponents the *soubriquet* of the 'tongues' movement.[1]

The Pentecostal Churches set immense value upon Christian experience of the Spirit, and indeed upon the expectation that it should be signified by profound emotion, and visibly and audibly expressed. Young Pentecostalists are taught to offer prayer in public, and thus learn a freedom in the realm of the spirit. Emphasis is laid upon the healing work of the Spirit, and our older readers will remember the healing missions of Pastor Jeffreys, founder of the Elim (centralised) branch of the movement, which was largely built up, originally in Wales, as a development of the Welsh Revival of 1904. The 'gift of tongues' is still experienced, and interpretation of tongues given. Perhaps the chief mark of these churches is a constant, confident and simple expectation that the promises of Scripture will be plainly fulfilled in this day and age. Whatever doubts may be entertained as to the balance and proportion of aspects of Pentecostalist teaching there can be little doubt that the followers of this way have a disturbing word for the more sophisticated and perhaps less expectant members of other Churches.

The Evangelical Witness

We have but sketched some few of the diverse ways in which the Evangelical movement is expressed outside the main body of our British Churches. In total the members of the Army citadels, the Brethren halls, and the churches of Elim and the Assemblies of God may seem to amount to a

[1] *The Pentecostal Movement* (Elim Publishing Co.), p. 7.

tiny proportion of even the church-going people of these islands, but their significance is greater than their numbers. They represent in separation elements which are present in the other Churches, like the strong Evangelical wing of the Church of England or the Baptists. But they also represent emphases which the main Churches have neglected. And their strength is far greater than their numbers suggest, since their members are customarily deeply committed to the work and worship of their fellowship, in ways that can but challenge those who would claim a more orthodox churchmanship. The whole Evangelical strand in British religion stresses the simple truth that no one, in Bishop Azariah's phrase, can be 'an hereditary Christian'.

8

THE CHURCHES COME TOGETHER

'I could never perceive any rational Consequence from those
many Texts which prohibit the Children of Israel to pollute
themselves with the Temples of the Heathens; we being all
Christians, and not divided by such detested impieties as might
prophane our prayers, or the place wherein we make them.'
Sir Thomas Browne, Religio Medici.

ON August 14, 1960, leaders of the Churches of the world
gathered in St Giles' Cathedral, Edinburgh, for a service of
thanksgiving for all that God had wrought for the unity of
his Church since fifty years ago the World Missionary Conference had met in that city. It is disturbing to reflect that
after fifty years the island within which that conference took
place could not show one single union of Churches belonging
to different confessional or denominational families. Earlier
pages have recorded two great acts of reunion within confessions. The reunion of the two large Churches of Scottish
Presbyterianism owes something directly to the vision and
stimulus of the conference held in 1910 within the Assembly
Hall of the United Free Church of Scotland. Indirectly the
conference had its effect upon the cause of Methodist reunion, although more influential forces were at work. In 1960
nonetheless there is hardly a serious hope of any act of
reunion in the next few years which would break through
the confessional barriers.

Many who came to St Giles for that jubilee act of thanksgiving could have pointed to achievements in the lands from
which they came. One of the prayers was offered by a leader
in the United Church of Canada, which as long ago as 1925

brought Methodists, Congregationalists and the majority of
Presbyterians into one Church in that dominion. In the
procession walked the General Secretary of the International
Missionary Council, Lesslie Newbigin, formerly a missionary
of the Church of Scotland and now wearing the saffron stole
of a bishop in the Church of South India. That Church in
1947 brought together Anglicans, Methodists and a former
union of Congregationalists and Presbyterians. That earlier
union in India took place in 1907. By contrast the conversations to achieve union between the Presbyterian Church of
England and the Congregational Union of England and Wales
after the Second World War failed (although a 'covenant'
relationship has been established, and there is, within wide
limits, mutual eligibility of ministers).

In many ways Britain has been at the heart of the movement for Christian co-operation and reunion. Not only was
that first of the great ecumenical conferences held in Scotland,
but its earliest result was the formation of the Conference of
Missionary Societies in Great Britain and Ireland in 1911.
Nine years later from the Lambeth Conference came the
famous 'Appeal to All Christian People'. The two conferences
of the Life and Work movement and the Faith and Order
movement in 1937 were held in Oxford and Edinburgh, and
it was in these gatherings that the determining decision was
taken to bring both together to form the World Council of
Churches. Britain has been exposed to ecumenical stimulus
to a remarkable degree.

Its contribution in leadership has been as striking.
Throughout the whole modern ecumenical movement a
Scotsman, Dr J. H. Oldham, has been 'God's back-room
boy', a pioneering mind ever driving the Churches out to the
demanding frontier with the contemporary world. The arch-
inspirer of the movement towards the World Council of
Churches was William Temple, successively Archbishop of
York, and, all too briefly, of Canterbury. An English Pres-

byterian minister, William Paton, was one of the chief creators of the network of national Christian councils within which the younger Churches have in many places come to maturity. George Bell, Bishop of Chichester, offered the capacious mind and heart that were needed to hold together in one person all the links that were gathering Christians in a world fellowship.

When these things are remembered the slow progress in these islands of Christian unity in its most demanding form seems hard to understand. It can only be accounted for in two ways. One is that while we certainly are in a missionary situation, as will have been constantly revealed in the by-going in our earlier chapters, it remains a disguised one. The provision of religious 'facilities' continues to be lavish. The schools and the BBC accept a duty of religious instruction. It is possible still to cling to the hope that the Churches might make a 'break through' into the whole of society again. (Not a little pathos attached to some support given to Dr Graham's campaigns, which derived from the sudden hope that there was a less demanding 'short cut' out of the Churches' present dilemma.) Certainly it has been the missionary imperative that has compelled union elsewhere. That imperative is still not strongly felt in Britain.

Another way in which we can account for the seeming gulf between the British share in the ecumenical movement and the paucity of solid results in Britain is to recognise that here, where many divisions take their origin, separate denominations still retain some residual meaning. One effect of setting out something of the background story in the preceding chapters is to enable us to recognise that these divisions are not just the result of the obstinacy of wayward and wilful men. They were more often the attempt to express new upsurges of religious experience, or fresh apprehensions of Christian truth. The obduracy of those in ecclesiastical power again and again compelled these new forces to be contained in separated bodies. 'Diversity is God's gift; division is what man does with it.' The effect of this is to give these divisions roots in our national life, or as we must more accurately say, our national *lives*. Students of recent discussions on unity in Scotland know that episcopacy is a concept not easily disentangled from thoughts and historical experiences of English aggression. Nor can anyone with knowledge of rural life of England doubt that the 'church' and 'chapel' distinction has both historical and sociological roots.

These are the brakes that are still on the wheels of the chariot of unity in Britain—an inadequately recognised missionary situation, and a remembrance of things past. But the chariot still moves.

Since 1942 there has been a definite instrument for Christian co-operation for almost all the Churches of the British Isles, save the Roman Catholic, in the British Council of Churches. In the course of its regular work a great number of the leaders of the Churches, both clerical and lay, are drawn together to consider issues in the realms of international affairs, education, social responsibility and so forth. The Youth Department is deeply engaged in a programme for giving ecumenical experience to the young men and women who will before long be carrying responsibility in their own congregations and denominations. Much more priority is now being given to faith and order questions in the Council's life, as a necessary corrective to a growing enterprise of common activity which might seem to accept our existing divisions, and even sanctify them by friendliness. And, immensely powerful in evoking widespread local commitment to ecumenical action, there is the Department of Inter-Church Aid and Refugee Service. Its Christian Aid Week each May has caused the churches to come together for Christian service in hundreds of areas in which there has been little before to draw them from a denominational to a wider Christian loyalty.

Associated with the British Council of Churches there are over 260 local Councils of Churches. They are chiefly in England. It is a small number still, albeit a steadily growing one. Few of them are dynamic centres of activity, but most of them are drawing the leaders of the churches locally into a greater knowledge and trust of one another.

The constant danger of the existence of these Councils is to lull us into forgetfulness that a plurality of churches in one place is an impossible concept to fit into the New Testament. Once, however, that danger is recognised and fought against, these instruments of co-operation serve as invaluable seed-beds for the growth of that understanding which must precede the more intrepid acts of unity.

The absence of any such prepared seed-bed in Scotland when the report on the conversations between Anglican and Presbyterian Churches was thrust into inhospitable soil in 1957 was all too obvious. Those who had participated in the conversations had long shared the process of working together and growing together. Those to whom the report was commended for study had known no comparable preparation. The conversations which are now proceeding between the Church of England and the Methodist Church have learned something from this lesson. Both by the production of an interim report, to enable members of the Churches involved to share something of the movement of thought in the representatives' minds, and by strong encouragement of increased fellowship between Anglican church and Methodist church at the parish level, the danger is being counteracted.

The reference to these reports reminds us that co-operation is not being seen as enough. Both these series of conversations result from the initiative of the then Archbishop, Dr Fisher, to which reference was made in our first chapter. His sermon preached before the University of Cambridge in November 1946 broke through the road-block which earlier inter-church conversations both between the Churches of England

and Scotland and between the Church of England and the Federal Council of the Evangelical Free Churches in the 1930's had frustratingly encountered. His basic suggestion was that the Free Churches should take episcopacy into their systems, and see how it worked within them. It is probably not unfair to say that the suggestion has proved on further examination at once unpalatable and inadequate. It has proved unpalatable to the Scottish Church for historical reasons. It has been felt to be inadequate for the reason that, after all the disturbance of traditions that this would involve to either Church of Scotland or an English Free Church, the fruit would be inter-communion rather than a union which would make one Church where there were two before. This has been recognised in the interim report on the Anglican-Methodist conversations, and full union is seen clearly as the goal to be attained.

Nevertheless it was the Archbishop's sermon which set things moving again, and, despite the set-back which the General Assembly of the Church of Scotland gave to the conversations between the Anglican and Presbyterian Churches in 1959 by declaring the proposals unacceptable, Dr Fisher proved undaunted. There is every prospect of continuing conversation, this time with the four participating Churches each having a larger body behind its few representatives for reference and consultation. This again is evidence that leaders now know that they cannot move too far ahead of the led.

Judgment varies enormously on the reaction to all this of the men and women who make up the British Churches. One judgment would affirm that left to themselves, without all these pernickety theologically-minded parsons, the laity would speedily achieve union all round. An exactly contrary one suggests that the ordinary layman is perplexed why his leaders are so bothered about bringing the Churches together, especially now we are all so friendly. Perhaps it is true to say that the increasing mobility of modern life causes many to sit more lightly to denominational allegiance, but once settled in a particular church people tend to resent being disturbed. Certainly, there is in England a great deal of crossing of denominational lines in suburb and housing estate between the Free Churches, and possibly more between Anglican and Free Churches than may be at first imagined. People looking for a 'live' church, or one that will be 'good for the children', are not good denominationalists. Diverse judgments, again, could be made of this phenomenon. We merely comment on its presence. The influence of the BBC in familiarising worshippers with other ways of devotion than their own may have contributed its share to it.

In one part of British church life there is a curious re-crudescence of denominational loyalties. Whereas in the earlier decades of this century it was in the Student Christian Movement in the universities that young Christians were first able to receive ecumenical experience (and many of today's senior leaders in the British Council of Churches and similar bodies were nurtured in that fellowship), today it is the denominational societies which hold the field there. As we have already noted, the Inter-Varsity Fellowship is strongly at work gathering a fellowship of the Evangelically like-minded. The SCM is still active in the colleges and univer-sities, and affords the only opportunity of that enlarging ecumenical experience for which a student should be eager. But in many universities the big numbers are to be found in the Anglican Society, the 'Meth-Soc', the 'Cong-Soc' and the like. The customary explanation for the simultaneous growth of the pan-confessional movements on a world scale with the growth of the ecumenical movement is hardly applicable here. It is usual to explain the new emphasis upon world Methodism or world Lutheranism as the inevitable reaction to ecumenical encounter. When you meet those of other traditions at close quarters you are forced into a denominational self-consciousness. 'Why am I what I am—a Baptist say, or an Anglican?' This hardly applies in the university to which young men and women come often with no experience of ecumenical encounter at all.

The explanation may lie in the fact that whereas the students at the universities earlier in the century came from secure and definite Christian backgrounds—and were thus ready for an adventurous foray—a great number of Christian students today are really first-generation Christians from non-churchgoing homes. They need the support of their own Church much more definitely. The Churches, too, recognising that situation, have been more active to appoint denominational chaplains. The effect of this has been to strengthen the denominational ethos for just that set of young men and women from which the movement towards Christian unity could reasonably have expected to recruit its new leaders. It is a situation fraught with questioning for the future.

Apart from a brief 'Indian Summer' of happier and closer relations between the Roman Catholic and other Churches during the tenure of the Archbishopric of Westminster by that great Englishman, Cardinal Arthur Hinsley, during the war years, there has been little development of bridges across that great divide. The speed with which the new Archbishop, Bernard Griffin, broke the tenuous links which had been forged revealed once again the difficulties of any co-operation with a Church of such exclusive convictions. The withdrawal some years later of all Roman Catholic officers from even the Council of Christians and Jews (at the express orders of the hierarchy, due to the alleged danger of 'indifferentism') confirmed non-Roman fears. Much more recently there has grown up some limited co-operation with Roman Catholics in the observance of the Week of Prayer for Christian Unity from January 18 to 25. Many Roman Catholics still observe it as the Octave of Unity with the Chair of St Peter, but there seems to be a growing number who are prepared to share in the true spirit of the Abbé Paul Couturier of Lyons who took the earlier observance and gave it a form in which all Christians could join without disloyalty to their convictions. While there is some suggestion that the British Roman hierarchy is apt to regard Couturierism as merely a Gallican heresy, often a Roman Catholic priest will prove prepared to share a common platform at a meeting in preparation for the Couturier observance, and some Roman parishes will give assurance of simultaneous prayer for 'that unity which Christ wills by the means which he chooses'.

A brief chapter like this can be little more than a hurried despatch from a front-line that is fortunately steadily moving forward. Our main tale in this book has been one of the great diversity of forms of Christian churchmanship to be found within these two small islands off the coast of Europe. What has happened here in the past has altered the Christian story of the world. Wherever the Anglican goes to Mattins, wherever a little Congregational church gathers to seek the mind of Christ, wherever Friends wait in silence for the movement of the Spirit, wherever the Salvationist dons his jersey or the Methodist sings the triumphant songs of Charles Wesley, British Christianity has left its original mark. World-wide communions have stemmed from obedience to the heavenly vision on English soil, and almost the whole family of English-speaking Presbyterian Churches looks back to the Scottish Kirk as a noble mother. An immense part of the oversea expansion of the Church in the past century and a half has sprung from the four countries that form the British isles. You may stand outside a Khasi church in the hills of Assam and hear the lilt caught from the Welsh hymn-singing of faithful missionaries from another mountainous land; or trace the journeys amidst the countless islands of the South Seas of the successive ships that have borne the name of John Williams and fitly expressed the missionary spirit of an island race.

The seed of the Word scattered on British soil, if often devoured by enmities, repelled by worldliness or received too lightly, has still in many parts of the world, by God's good grace, brought forth an hundredfold.

Slack, Kenneth.
The British churches today. London, SCM Press [1961]
176p. 19cm. (SCM paperback)

1.Sects-Gt. Brit. 2.Gt. Brit.-Religion. I.Title.